Small Scale Entrepreneurship

Small Scale Entrepreneurship

Dr. K. Lavanya Latha
MBA., Ph.D.
Assistant Professor
Dept. of Business Administration
Yogi Vemana University
Kadapa-516003

SERIALS PUBLICATIONS
NEW DELHI (INDIA)

First Published - 2010

ISBN: 978-81-8387-377-2

Published by

SERIALS PUBLICATIONS
4830/24, Prahlad Street, Ansari Road
Darya Ganj, New Delhi-110002 (India)
Phone : 23245225 Fax : 91-11-23272135
E-mail: serials@satyam.net.in

Dedicated to

My Beloved Parents

Sri. K. Gopi & Smt. K. Subbalakshmi

CONTENTS

PREFACE

The economic development and prosperity of any region largely depends on the demographic composition and quality of its people. If they are sincere, enterprising, ambitious and innovative to bear the risks, the region will develop. Such people are identified as entrepreneurs. Entrepreneurs are not born, it is the environment, training, family tradition and circumstances which help development and promotion of successful entrepreneurs. Both the developed and underdeveloped countries look at the industrialization process as an important key to economic development . The availability of entrepreneurship is today, widely accepted as the most important determinant in the process of industrialization. Infect, one of the most important reasons for the poor economic growth of our country has been the lack of entrepreneurship among the people.

The present study is an attempt to analyze the growth and development of small scale entrepreneurship in a backward region of the country, namely, Nellore district of Andhra Pradesh. It is needless to emphasize here that in a backward region like Nellore district, the relevance of small scale entrepreneurship development to the over all economic development of the region is quite essential. To be precise, this study aims at studying the socio-economic factors, motivational factors, growth factors, impact of globalization and liberalization and the problems faced by the small scale entrepreneurs.

This study consists of five chapters. The First chapter highlights the importance of research, presents the background of the study, the need for the study, statement of the problem and objectives of the study. The Second chapter reviews of the related literature of small scale entrepreneurship in abroad, India and Andhra Pradesh. The Third chapter addresses the methodology and design used in the study. It deals with sampling frame, research questions, data collection, procedure and method of data analysis. The Fourth chapter is concerned with the state of Indian economy, Andhra Pradesh and Nellore district. The Fifth chapter presents the analysis of the data collected from 196 small scale entrepreneurs through questionnaires, together with findings. The last chapter sums up the conclusions that emerged from the study, offers necessary suggestions for improving the small scale enterprises and directions for future research.

Dr. K. LAVANYA LATHA

ACKNOWLEDGEMENT

This work originated under the scholarly guidance of my teacher and Principal Director of Research, Prof. B.E.V.V.N. Murthy, Ex-Dean and Professor, School of Commerce, Management and Information Sciences, Sri Venkateswara University, Tirupati. It has been my privilege and pleasure to work under his expert supervision. His dedication towards academic pursuits has always been a source of inspiration to me. But for his care, inducement and personal affection, this task would not have come to its successful completion. I am short of words to express my gratitude to him

I would like to take the opportunity of acknowledging my deep sense of gratitude to Prof. T. Siddaiah, Principal, Dr. M. Srinivasa Reddy, Head, Prof. C.G. Krishnamacharyulu, Prof. S. Balarama Reddy, Dr. S. Durga Rao, Dr. B. Sudhir, Dr. D.V. Ramana, Dr. P. Balaji Prasad Dr. P. Raghunathadha Reddy and Dr. B. Suresh Rao, Department of Management Studies, Sri Venkateswara University, Tirupati for their incessant encouragement and inspiration to pursue the academic work of high standard.

The present research work, being first of its kind would have been impossible without the co-operation of the entrepreneurs, who spared their most valuable time to supply necessary information in response to my lengthy questionnaire. To acknowledge them individually is however, difficult for want of space, but I am really very grateful to all of them, and any amount of expression would be totally inadequate.

I am particularly grateful to Prof. A. Papa Rao, Department of Anthropology and Prof. B. Mohan, Prof. D. Himachalam, Department of Commerce who stood as a tower of strength and made many useful suggestions in improving this work. I am thankful to many friends who offered encouragement and courage during the progress of the work.

Last, but not the least, a very special thanks to my life partner Dr. K. Prabhakar, my parents, my sisters, K.K.C. Deepthi and K. Sahana who kept on encouraging and reminding me of the challenges of the work. Their moral support, affectionate concern for my prosperity and well being has greatly helped in completion of this book.

Dr. K. LAVANYA LATHA

1

INTRODUCTION

BACKGROUND OF THE STUDY

Entrepreneurship in India plays a catalytic and important role in the economic development. It has emerged as a dynamic and vibrant sector of the economy. It is a well recognized fact that a vibrant entrepreneurship holds the key to economic prosperity in an economy characterized by abundant labour supply, unemployment and underemployment, capital scarcity, growing modern large industrial sector giving scope for ancillarisation and so on. Entrepreneurship has grown phenomenally during the past five decades besides playing a vital role in the fulfilling of our socio-economic objectives.

Entrepreneurship has developed in a systematic way since the beginning of Industrial Revolution in Europe. The development of entrepreneurship is essential for rapid economic development and has engaged the attention of economists, sociologists, and psychologists to study the phenomenon in the developed and developing countries in recent years. Consequently, the phenomenon of entrepreneurship has been viewed from these three dimensions. The research studies in the field of entrepreneurship by an individual, or a group have contributed largely to the formation of various theoretical framework for analyzing entrepreneurial behaviour, however, these studies have been influenced by the particular discipline to which the individual or the group belongs. There has not been any monolithic approach towards theory-building in the field of entrepreneurial development. Various scholars have highlighted multiple approach to the study of entrepreneurial behaviour and entrepreneurship. A scholar of economics tends to emphasize the economic aspects of entrepreneurship, a sociologist analyses in terms of socio-cultural environment, values and family tradition, whereas a psychologist highlights personality factor of entrepreneurship. No single factor therefore works as the only determining variable for the phenomenon of entrepreneurship. However, the theoreticians have made and have been making some efforts to bring out some single factor as the dominant one to analyse entrepreneurship.

The concept of "entrepreneur" and the "entrepreneurship" have gone through various stages before they came to signify the content being put into them now. Various thinkers have defined the term in a variety of ways. In order to understand the phenomenon of entrepreneurship as whole, it is worthwhile to analyse these definitions and views independently.

The word "entrepreneur" is derived from the French verb "entreprendre", means "to undertake". The word entrepreneur has been in use since the sixteenth century. Kilby has linked the entrepreneur with a rather large and very important animal called "Heffalump" hunted by many individuals and have variously described him, but wide disagreements still exist among them on his particularities[1]. The French men who organized and led military expeditions were referred to as "entrepreneurs"[2].

Around 1700 A.D., the term was used for architects and contractors of public works. Quesnay regarded the rich farmer as an "entrepreneur" who manages and makes his business profitable by his intelligence, skill and wealth[3].

In the 18th century, the old Oxford Dictionary of 1897 defined entrepreneur simply as "the director or manager of public musical institution, i.e., one who 'gets up' entertainments, especially musical performance"[4]. The dictionary in its supplement of 1933 modified its definition and recognized that the word has a place in business; it defines entrepreneur as one who undertakes an enterprise[5], especially a contractor acting as an intermediary between capital and labour. Undertaking an enterprise is entrepreneurship, and one who undertakes it is one who combines capital and labour for the purpose of production is an entrepreneur.

The concept of entrepreneur has many facets and the term has been used in a different context with a different perspective. Economists have recognized the entrepreneur as essential agent in generating investment opportunities. Sociologists analyse him as sensitive energizer in modernization of societies. The psychologists examine him as an "entrepreneurial man", his motivations and aspirations in order to decipher his character which is conducive to economic development. Political scientists regard him as the fair child of political system which provides effective assistance for his emergence[6].

In economic theories, the concept of entrepreneur has been coined in terms of functions. Richard Cantillon, an Irishman living in France, was the first person to introduce the term 'entrepreneur', in the early 18th Century. He defined entrepreneur as an agent who buys factors of production at certain prices in order to combine them into a product with a view to selling it at uncertain prices in future[7]. Cantillon emphasized the function of 'risk-taking' and 'uncertainly bearing'. He illustrates the concept by giving examples of farmers, manufacturers and traders. The risk and uncertainty is inherent in these activities. Since Cantillon has stressed one aspect of the concept, he could not enjoy economic popularity for a long time.

Frank H. Knight defined the entrepreneur, more or less, similar to those of Cantillon. Uncertainty is defined as a risk which cannot be insured against and is incalculable. According to him, entrepreneur is an economic functionary who undertakes such responsibility of uncertainty which by its very nature cannot be insured, or capitalized or salaried. He also guarantees certain sums to other means in return for assignments made to them. According to him, the supply of entrepreneurship involves three factors: ability, willingness, and power to extend such guarantee[8].

Jean Baptiste Say, an aristocratic industrialist, and a French economist, developed the concept of entrepreneur a little further. He emphasized the functions of co-ordination, organization and supervision. In more simple words, an entrepreneur is one, who combines the land of the one, labour of another, and the capital of yet another and thus, produces a product. By selling the produce in the market he/she pays interest on capital, rent on land, wages to labours and what remains is his/her profit[9]. According to J.B. Say, the entrepreneur is an organizer and speculator of a business enterprise, who combines economic resources out of an area of lower into an area of higher productivity and greater yield. He has clearly distinguished between the role of a capitalist as a financier and of an entrepreneur as an organizer of a business activity.

Say, Mill[10] and Marshall[11] emphasized the role of entrepreneur as an organizer and recognized the entrepreneur as the central figure in a business enterprise, however according to the critics, they failed to see full significance of the role of an entrepreneur of which combining factors of production is only one aspect.

The concept of entrepreneur propagated by all the above thinkers was in the context of static conditions, and was not related to the process of economic development.

Joseph Alois Schumpeter, for the first time, in 1934, assigned a crucial role of 'innovation' to the entrepreneur in his 'magnum opuses, the theory of 'economic development'[12]. Schumpeter considered economic development as discrete dynamic change. Such discontinuous dynamic changes are brought about by entrepreneur by instituting new combinations of the factors of production, i.e., 'innovation'[13].

Innovation may take place in the following forms:

(i) The introduction of a new product in the market.

(ii) The instituting of a new production technology which is not yet tested by experience in the branch of manufacturing concerned.

(iii) The opening of new market into which the specific product has not been previously introduced.

(iv) The discovery of a new source of supply of raw material.

(v) The carrying out of the new form of organization of any industry like the creation of monopoly position or the breaking up of it[14].

Schumpeter further distinguished between invention and innovation. An inventor discover a new method and new materials, and an innovator utilizes inventions and discoveries in order to make new combinations and thus produces newer and better goods which yield him profit and satisfaction. The inventor produces ideas and the entrepreneur implements them. He considered innovation as creative response to a situation.

Schumpeter's concept of 'entrepreneur' is very wide, in the sense, he includes not only independent businessmen but also to some extent, dependent employees of a firm like managers, directors and so on, provided they do innovative work. On the other side, the definition is narrow, because it does not include industrialists and employees who operate an established concern. According to him no one is permanently an entrepreneur so long as he gives creative and innovative response to market situation. He, while emphasizing the innovative function of an entrepreneur, ignored his risk-bearing function which is equally important.

Schumpeter wrote his theory of economic development in the context of Industrial Revolution of presently advanced countries where some of the pre-requisites of growth already existed. Inevitably, his theoretical explanation corresponds to a particular social and economic order that existed there during that specific period. Innovation was concentrated in a few fields in which big entrepreneurs rose as the spearheads of growth. Big innovations yielded a surplus for reinvestment and in this way the entrepreneur could invade the various economic fields with spectacular success[15].

The applicability of the Schumpeterian 'innovative' concept of entrepreneur to underdeveloped economies is conditioned on the above grounds. Things are likely to be different in underdeveloped or developing countries. In such situations, entrepreneurs have to face numerous problems like imperfect market, shortages of capital, of skilled labour and of technical know how. Against these odds they are required to develop their industries. Naturally they cannot reach the scale of operation visualized by Schumpeter. But it does not prove that entrepreneur in underdeveloped or developing countries requires any less ability and ingenuity. The business leader in underdeveloped countries can also be called an entrepreneur.

Peter Drucker defines an 'entrepreneur' as one who always searches for change, responds to it, and exploits it as an opportunity, entrepreneurs innovate. Drucker has aptly observed that 'innovation' is the specific tool of entrepreneurs, the means by which they exploit changes as an opportunity for a different business or a different service. It is capable of being presented as a discipline, capable of being learned, capable of being practised. Entrepreneurs need to search purposefully for the source of innovation, the changes and their symptoms that indicate opportunities for successful innovation. And they need to know and to apply the principle of successful innovation[16].

According to Drucker, three conditions have to be fulfilled:

1. Innovation is a work. It requires knowledge. It often requires great ingenuity. It makes great demands on diligence, persistence and commitment.
2. To succeed, innovation must build on its own strength.
3. Innovation has to be close to the market, focused on the market, indeed market-driven.

According to Francis A. Walker, the true entrepreneur is one who is endowed with more than average capacities in the task of organizing and coordinating the various other factors of production. He should be a pioneer and captain of an industry. The supply of such entrepreneurship is however quite limited and enterprise in general consists of several grades of organizational skill and capability. The more efficient entrepreneurs receive a surplus reward over and above the managerial wages and this sum constitutes trade profit ascribed to superior talent[17].

The above definitions specified by different thinkers, stress only selected aspects of entrepreneurship. In modern times, an attempt is made to generate a comprehensive definition which tries to highlight all facets and aspects of entrepreneurial activity. These multidimensional aspects may be stated as follows to frame synthesized concept of entrepreneur. In an enterprise, land, labour and capital are separately owned respectively by landowners, labours and financiers and are divorced from one another. An entrepreneur is an organizer, his organizing ability brings them together in proper proportions at reasonable rates and harnesses them to work in production, attempts to produce a socially valuable product, so as to yield the best returns. As an organizer, he also guarantees the specific sums to the landowners, labours and financiers in return for assignments made to them. An entrepreneur bears the risk which is inherent in any business activity. An entrepreneur starts the enterprise, organizes it, supervises it and engineers long-run plan of the enterprise. He is a specially motivated and talented person, who implements new ideas, visualizes opportunities for introducing new products, techniques, and production process, new form of organization, discovers new market and new source of supply of raw materials. That is how, he innovates, and in this way he takes upon himself the entire responsibility of the enterprise.

According to B.C.Tandon[18], entrepreneurship means the composite function of creating something new, organizing and co-ordinating and undertaking risk and handling economic uncertainty. In this context, an entrepreneur is the person who tries to create something new, organizes production and undertakes risk and handles economic uncertainty involved in enterprise.

In the same context, the definition of Higgins seems to be worth quoting, "Entrepreneurship" is meant the function of seeing investment and production opportunities, organizing an enterprise to undertake a new production process, raising capital, hiring labour, arranging for a supply of raw materials and finding site, and combining these factors of production into a going concern; introducing new techniques and commodities, discovering new sources of natural resources; and selecting top managers for day-to-day operations of the enterprise[19].

According to William Diamond, "Entrepreneurship is equivalent to 'enterprise' which 'involves the willingness to assume risks in undertaking an economic activity, particularly a new one. It may involve an innovation but not necessarily so. It always involves risk-taking, decision-making, although neither risk nor decision making may be of great significance [20].

Entrepreneurship refers to a process of action, an entrepreneur (person) undertakes to establish the enterprise. The term 'entrepreneur' has been defined as one who detects and evaluates a new situation in his environment and directs the making of such adjustments in the economic systems as he deems necessary. He conceives of an industrial enterprise for the purpose of, displays considerable initiative, goal and determination in bringing his project to fruition, and in this process, performs one or more of the following:

(i) perceives opportunities for profitable investments;

(ii) explores the prospects of starting such a manufacturing enterprise;

(iii) obtains necessary industrial licences;

(iv) arranges initial capital;

(v) provides personal guarantees to the financial institutions;

(vi) promises to meet the shortfalls in the capital; and

(vii) supplied technical know-how[21].

The entrepreneurs' role is to furnish technical skills, commercial knowledge and powers of administration, to assume responsibilities and provide against contingencies, to share and direct production and organize and control the industrial machine[22]. Entrepreneurs are people who have the ability to see and evaluate business opportunities to gather the necessary resources to take advantage of them and to initiate appropriate action to ensure success[23].

Psychological stress is a natural concomitance of any creative activity. It is much more so if the activity relates to an intensely competitive area like business. Entrepreneurs, being creative individuals, often experience such stress at various stages of development of their enterprises[24].

Marbinson's entrepreneur is not an innovator but an organization builder who must be able to harness the new ideas of different innovators to the rest of the organisation[25].

In modern context, the term 'entrepreneur' has been used in a broader perspective. According to Vasant Desai [26] the entrepreneur brings in overall change through innovation for the maximum social good. Further, India which itself is an underdeveloped country aims at decentralized industrial structure to mitigate the regional imbalances in levels of economic development, small scale entrepreneurship in such industrial structure plays an important role to achieve balanced regional development[27].

Lastly, the establishment of Entrepreneurship Development Institute, various developmental policies and alike by the Indian Government during the last five decades bear a good testimony to her strong realization about the premium role of entrepreneurship played in economic development.

In the light of above, the present study attempts to study the growth and developmental factors for small scale entrepreneurship. This study also attempts to get the insights to study the motivational factors behind the entrepreneur that motivated to go for entrepreneurship and also problems faced by the entrepreneurs. The coastal district of Nellore in Andhra Pradesh state has been selected as the geographical area of the study.

Before presenting the purpose and objectives of the study as well as the specific research questions, it would be appropriate to have an overview of small scale entrepreneurship in the country, its role and importance, and the nature of the general problems and challenges faced.

OVERVIEW OF SMALL SCALE ENTREPRENEURSHIP IN INDIA

Entrepreneurship is regarded as one closely associated with economic history of India. The evolution of the Indian entrepreneurship can be traced back to even as early as Rigveda, when metal handicrafts existed in the society[28]. This would bring the point home that handicrafts entrepreneurship in India was as old as the human civilization itself and was nurtured by the craftsmen as a part of their duty towards the society. Before India came into contact with the west, people were organized in a particular type of economic and social system of the village community. The Indian towns were mostly religious and the elaborated caste based diversion of workers consisted of farmers, artisans and religious priests (the Brahmins). The majority of the artisans were treated as village servants. Such compact system of village community, effectively protecting village artisans from the onslaughts of external competition, was one of the important contributing factors to the absence of localization of industry in ancient India[29]. Organized industrial activity was observable among the Indian artisans in a few recognizable products in the cities of Banaras, Allahabad, Gaya, Puri and Mirzapur which were established on their river basins as a means of transportation facilities. Bengal enjoyed worldwide celebrity for corah, Lucknow for chintzes, Ahmedabad for dupattas and dhotis, Nagpur for silk-bordered clothes, Kashmir for shawls and Banaras for metal wares. Thus till the earlier years of the eighteenth century, India enjoyed the prestigious status of the queen of the International trade with the help of its handicrafts.

Unfortunately, so much prestigious Indian handicrafts industry, which was basically a cottage and small sector, declined at the end of the eighteenth century for various reasons like disappearance of the Indian Royal courts and entry of British people with the competition of machine-made goods[30]. The emergence of manufacturing entrepreneurship can be noticed in the second half of the nineteenth century. Ranchodlal chotalal, a Nagar Brahman, was the first Indian to think of setting up the textile manufacturing on the modern factory lines in 1847, but failed. In his second attempt, he succeeded in setting up a textile mill in 1861 in Ahmedabad[31]. But before this, the first cotton textile–manufacturing unit was already set up by a Parsi, Cowasjee Nanabhoy Davar in Bombay in 1854 followed by Nawrosjee Wadia, who opened his textile mill in Bombay in 1880. Probably the major Indian contribution in the Nineteenth century came in the field of banking, where every important company owned its existence, in part, to the enterprise and capital of Indians[32]. A few beginnings were made by Indians in heavy industries–steel, engineering, electric power and shipping[33] in the early part of the twentieth country. The most spectacular of these ventures was by Jamshedjee Tata, a Parsi, who was responsible for India's first viable steel enterprise in Jamshedpur in 1911. The Swadeshi Campaign i.e., emphasis on indigenous goods, provided, indeed a proper seed bed for inculcating and developing nationalism in the country. It was the influence of Swadeshi that Jamshedji Tata even named his first mill as "Swadeshi Mill". The spirit of indigenousness strengthened its roots so much in the country that the Krishna Mills in its advertisement of Tribune of April 13 made the following appeal "Our concern is financed by native capital and is under native management throughout[34]. The second wave of entrepreneurship growth in India began after the First World War. The government gave mild protection and some encouragement to the select forms of enterprise, especially sugar and cement. By 1939, there were 11,114 companies (not all of them industrial concerns) which were mostly functioning in and around Bombay,

Calcutta and Ahmedabad with a capital investment of Rs. 290 crores. In 1945, the number of companies had gone up to 14,859 and the capital investment had risen to Rs. 9 crores[35]. The development that took place did not bring about either a degree of regional balance or major structural changes in the Indian economy. The entrepreneurs who contributed to this development were mostly drawn from the well known business houses and families such as Birla, Tata, Dalmia–Jain, Bangur and Thapar[36]. In the post 1990, the new class of entrepreneurs like Dhirubhai Ambany of Reliance, Brijmohanlal of Hero Honda, Anji Reddy of Dr.Reddy Lab, Narayana Murthy of Infosys, Azim Premji of Wipro, Ramalingaraju of Satyam Computers and many more have taken the country as one among the most preferred countries for investment in the world. There are about 2542 listed companies in the Bombay Stock Exchange. The market capitalization of the traded companies on Bombay Stock Exchange is Rs. 22,51,012 Crores[37].

India relies mostly on the performance of agricultural and industrial sectors for their economic development. The agricultural sector has a vast employment potential but is unable to absorb the fast multiplying population. This situation calls for developing alternatives to meet the needs of ever growing population. So our planners and economists focused attention on accelerating the economic growth through rapid entrepreneurship in the present era. In fact the small scale entrepreneurship has been assigned high priority in the development of economy of the country. Entrepreneurs contributed relatively more in a society, which had free economy and provided high prestige and security to entrepreneurs than the one, which had relatively more regulated economy and provided lesser prestige and security.

When India attained Independence, the new government began to realize the need for accelerating industrial development and a general protectionist system was introduced. Consequently, the various Industrial Policies provided major guidelines for industrial development and at the same time the government started to provide various incentives and concessions in the form of capitalist, technical know–how, markets and land to the potential entrepreneurs to establish industries in the industrially potential areas to remove the regional imbalances in development. The Five Year Plans provided the necessary frame work through their specific programme for economic development of the nation. Several institutions like Small Industries Development Organization, National Small Industries Corporation, Small Industries Service Institutes at the Central Government and Directorate of Industries, Financial Corporations, Small Scale Industries Board, District Industries Centres were also established by the State Government to facilitate the new entrepreneurs in setting up their enterprises. Expectedly, the Small Scale Units emerged very rapidly in India witnessing a tremendous increase in their number from 121,619 in 1966 to 190,727 in 1970 registering an increase of 17,000 units per year during the period under reference. The family entrepreneurship units like Tatas, Birlas, Mafatlals, Dalmias, Kirloskars, Ambanies, Brijmohanlals, Narayana Murthy, Azim Premji and others grew beyond the normally expected size and also established new frontiers in business in this period. District Industries Centres at the district level functioned as nodal centres for development of small scale entrepreneurship in rural and semi urban areas. District Industries Centres operated as 'single window' agency through which all assistance needed for small scale entrepreneurship were streamlined. List of products reserved for small industries increased dramatically from 180 to 540 and later to 812. The Third Census of small scale industries reveals that the total number of small scale industries has increased from 79.6 lakhs in 1994-95 to 110.10 lakhs in 2002-03, indicating an annual average growth rate of 4.1 percent, 12.4 percent production and exports recorded a growth rate of 14.5 percent[38]. On the other hand, industrial licensing, price controls, administrative restrictions and regulations, and a highly progressive tax rate on income and wealth hampered domestic entrepreneurship. Small scale entrepreneurship also facilitated removal of regional disparity in business. The items from a paper pin to technology–based products were manufactured in the sector and the units were dispersed in districts, towns and villages all over the country. Thus there was a significant growth of small scale enterprise population, their production and employment, besides contributing to a major share of country's exports.

NEED FOR THE STUDY

Entrepreneurship helps in the industrialization of the country in different ways viz., assembling and harnessing the various inputs, bearing the risks, innovating and imitating the techniques of production to reduce the cost and increase the quality and quantity, expanding the horizons of the market and coordinating and managing the manufacturing unit at various levels. In fact, the industrial development of a country crucially depends upon the number and abilities of its entrepreneurs. Entrepreneurship, therefore, is regarded as one of the determining factors of the industrial growth of a country.

The problem of underdevelopment has different dimensions in the different parts of India. This problem becomes still more complex in the backward districts like Nellore. Nellore is one of the industrially backward districts of the state of Andhra Pradesh placed under the 'C' category by the Central Government inspite of its proximity to the industrial belt of Chennai and availability of railway heads, 180kms of national highways, the district has lagged behind in industrial development. The Nellore municipality has been upgraded as a corporation by the Government of Andhra Pradesh on 8th October, 2004.

Therefore, the need to support the development of small scale entrepreneurship is more in case of units established in the backward regions than those coming up in the advanced regions of the country. Nellore district is such a backward region that needs special study for the policy formulation that will enable the state to grow industrially. It is needless to emphaze here that in a backward district like Nellore, the relevance of small scale entrepreneurship to the economic development of the state is beyond doubt.

Therefore, any attempt to study the nature of development of small scale industries should include the areas such as the present development trend in the growth of small scale industries, the nature and characteristics of entrepreneurial orientation and impact of globalization and liberalization to the small enterprises. This, we believe, will reflect the deficiency if any, in the process of development of this sector as a whole.

For the development of the small scale entrepreneurship in the state the problems relating to marketing, provision for adequate credit etc., have to be studied properly. Moreover, these hurdles have to be overcome with the coordinated efforts of the government, financial institutions and the small entrepreneurs concerned. Therefore, our study on growth and development of entrepreneurship is based on the analysis so as to find out the socio–economic and motivational factors of the entrepreneurs, growth and developmental factors, impact of globalization and liberalization on small scale entrepreneurship and whether the small entrepreneurs themselves operate their units successfully despite the existence of several problems.

STATEMENT OF THE PROBLEM

In spite of the fact that small scale entrepreneurship has a long history of development and its importance in national economic scene is steadily growing, there is very little literature providing an objective assessment of small scale entrepreneurship. The literature, available in mostly government reports and more often than not studies by administration involved in formulation of policies for its implementation. This kind of literature is likely to lack objectivity and impartial assessment of the role of small scale entrepreneurship in the country.

This observation is more relevant in the context of small scale entrepreneurship in the district of Nellore, whose exact place of importance in the overall economic system and the direction of growth are not properly assessed. In view of the fact that small scale entrepreneurship has come to occupy a pivotal role, a study about the nature of entrepreneurship, development trends in terms of number of units, employment and investment, incentives and assistance, besides financial; may be meaningful and purposive. The study, to begin with, analyses the growth and developmental factors of this sector over certain period, the factors responsible for entrepreneurial motivation, opinion of entrepreneurs regarding impact of globalization and liberalization on the small scale entrepreneurship. With this analysis, an attempt is made to identify their problems which would go a long way in helping, suggest the future policies and remove hurdles restraining their growth and development.

OBJECTIVES OF THE STUDY

The objectives of the study are

1. To find out the socio-economic characteristics of entrepreneurs.
2. To probe the factors that motivated the entrepreneurs.
3. To ascertain the factors that contribute to the growth of entrepreneurship.
4. To study the impact of globalization and liberalization on the growth of entrepreneurship.
5. To identify the problems faced by the entrepreneurs.
6. To give suggestions to promote entrepreneurship.

ORGANISATION OF THE THESIS

This thesis is organized into six chapters. The chapter sequence and the topics dealt with are as follows.

The First chapter, "Introduction", introduces the topic of research, initially presenting the background of the study. An overview of Growth and Development of Small Scale Entrepreneurship, its role and economic development are dealt with. The need for the study, statement of problem and objectives of the study are presented.

The Second chapter, "Review of Literature" presents the review of the related literature in the fields of small scale entrepreneurship. The literature review includes the concepts and theoretical under pinning relevant to the topic of small scale entrepreneurship. This sections deals with studies of entrepreneurship in abroad, India and Andhra Pradesh. The brief findings from the review of previous research work on small scale entrepreneurship provided the basis for statement of problem and research topic.

The chapter Three, "Research Methodology", addresses the methodology and design used in the study. The sections of this chapter deal with sampling frame and samples, research questions, measures used, data collection and procedure, and method of data analysis. This study is based on survey method. From the angle of the purpose of the study, this is mainly of descriptive type.

The chapter Four deals with, "Socio–economic Profile of the Study Region". The study was conducted in Nellore district of Andhra Pradesh State. The chapter presents the state of Indian economy, Andhra Pradesh economy and the district economy, in particular, the status of development of small scale entrepreneurship, and the availability of infrastructure. This chapter is relevant because the topic of study involves socio-economic background of small scale entrepreneurship. The study of economic and social environment is considered useful for analysis of the research data.

The chapter Five, 'Analysis of Determinants of Growth and Development of Entrepreneurship' presents the analysis of the data collected from 196 small enterprises through survey questionnaires, together with findings that resulted from the survey. It has sections containing (i) analysis of general information and background. (ii) enterprise start up data analysis and the

(iii) socio–economic factors analysis. The sections thereafter are specific to motivational factor's analysis. The analysis of growth factors of small scale entrepreneurs is made and current problems of entrepreneurs are presented. The section presents impact of globalization and liberalization on small scale entrepreneurs. Together with the analysis of opinions on entrepreneurs success is presented.

The chapter Six, 'Summary of Findings and Suggestions', the results are presented. The last section presents the conclusions based on the findings of the study. Besides, a few specific suggestions for small scale entrepreneurs as well as suggestions for policy makers, concerned with small scale entrepreneurship development, have been presented. The chapter concludes with directions for future research.

SUMMARY

In conclusion, this chapter presents background of the study and its importance in economic development of the country. Besides, an overview of small scale entrepreneurship in India is presented to understand its growth and development.

While reviewing the literature, some gaps were noticed and the need for the study along with the statement of the problem for choosing the research area 'Nellore district' is presented. These gaps motivated the researcher to undertake an indepth research study and objectives of the study are presented. Lastly organization of this thesis is presented. The review of literature is described in the next chapter.

REFERENCES

1. Peter Kilbly (1971), "Hunting the Heffalump": Entrepreneurship and Economic Development (ed.,), The Free Press, New York,p. 1-40.
2. Richard A. Peterson (1962), Entrepreneurship and Economic Development, Vol. XII -2, p.65.
3. Vasant Desai (1991), Entrepreneurial Development, Himalaya Publishing House, Vol. 1, Bombay, p.30.

4. Tandon. B.C. (1975), Environment and Entrepreneur, Chugh Publication, Allahabad, p.53.

5. *Ibid.*, p.33.

6. Shravanvel. P. (1987), Entrepreneurial Development: Principles, Policies and Programmes, Ess-Pee-Kay Publishing House, Madras, p.21.

7. Peter Kibly (1971), op.cit., p.2.

8. Knight, H.Frank (1957), Risk Uncertainty and Profit, Houghton Muffin Company, Chapter VII-XI, New York.

9. Say, J.B. (1815), "Catheism of Political Economy", London Sherwood, p.28-29.

10. Tondon, B.C. (1971), op.cit., p.2.

11. Mershall, A. (1961), Principle of Economics: An Introductory Volume, The English Language Book Society and MacMillan, London, p.244.

12. Joseph Alois Schumpeter (1934), The Theories of Economic Development, Translated by R.Opie Cambridge, Harvard University Press, p.66, 74-90.

13. Joseph Alois Schumpeter (1939), Business Cycle, Mc Graw Hill Book Company, New York, p.103.

14. Bisht, N.S. et.al., (1989), Entrepreneurship Reflections and Investigations (Ed.)., Chugh Publication, Allahabad, p. 23-24.

15 Singh Pritam (1966), The Role of Entrepreneurship in Economic Development: Issues and Policies, Butani and Singh (Ed), Vora and Co., Bombay, p.228.

16. Vasant Desai, op.cit., p.32.

17. Shravanvel, op.cit., p.25.

18. Tandon, B.C, op.cit., p.38.

19. Benjamin Higgins (1961), Economic Development, Central Book Depot, Allahabad, p.88.

20. William Diamond (1957), Development Bank, The John Hopkins Press, Baltimore, p.5.

21. Clarence H.Danhof, (1949), Observations of Entrepreneurship in Agriculture and the Entrepreneurs, Harvard University Press, England, p.35.

22. Francis Walker (1986), The Wages Question, Henry Holt, New York,p. 245.

23. Geoffrey G. Meredith, Robert E. Nelson, Philip A Neck, (1982), "The Practice of Entrepreneurship", International Labour Office, Genera, p.3.

24. Udai Pareek and T.V. Rao (1995), Counselling and Helping Entrepreneurs, The Journal of Entrepreneurship, Vol.4, January-June, p.19.

25. Frederick, H. (1956), Entrepreneurial Organization: As a Factor in Economic Development, Quarterly Journal of Economics, Vol. LXX, No.3, August, p.364-368.

26. Vasant Desai (2004), "Dynamics of Entrepreneurial Development and Management", Himalaya Publishing House, New Delhi, p.17.

27. Khanka S.S. (1994), Industrial Development of Backward Areas, Himalaya Publishing House, New Delhi, p.86.

28. Rao R.V. (1969), Indian Handicrafts, Bookhamas Private Limited, Hyderabad, p.10.

29. Deshpande M.U. (1984), Entrepreneurship of Small Scale Industries, Deep & Deep Publications, New Delhi, p.63.

30. Gadgil D.R. (1959), The Industrial Evolution of India in Recent Times (1860–1939), Oxford University Press, London, p.36.

31. Howard Spodak (1965), The Manchestrisation of Ahmedabad, The Economic Weekly, 17 (11), March 13, p.483.

32. Radha Shyam Rungta (1970), " The Rise of Business Corporations in India", 1851–1900, Cambridge University Press.

33. Helen, B Lamb (1955), " The Rise of Indian Business Communities", Pacific Affairs, 23, No. 2., June, p.105.

34. Arun Joshi, Lala Shri Ram (1975), A Study in Entrepreneurship & Industrial Management, Orient Longman, New Delhi.

35. Some Notes towards a Theory of Derived Development in the Economics of Underdevelopment, Ed., A.N. Agrawala & S.P.Singh, p.193.

36. Hozari, R.K. (1965), The Structure of Corporate Sector, Asia Publications House Bombay.

37. The Economic Times (2005), 8th November.

38. Ruddar Dutt and Sundharam, K.P.M. (2006), Indian Economy, S.Chand & Company Publications, New Delhi, p.683.

2

REVIEW OF LITERATURE

INTRODUCTION

This chapter presents the conceptual and theoretical under pinning that is relevant to this research study. The first few sections of the chapter discuss the definition and concepts of small enterprises. The latter sections deal with entrepreneurship and entrepreneurial studies carried out in abroad, India and Andhra Pradesh. The chapter concludes with identification of gaps in the existing literature and identifying the research problem.

The study of literature published in the subject area, facilitates the researcher to understand the growth and development of the same. It also helps to identify the grey areas and the areas that need further research. In order to achieve the objectives of the present study an extensive review of literature was carried out, focusing on small scale entrepreneurship, in developed and developing countries.

At macro level small enterprises provide a foundation for economic development of the country. But at micro level, a small enterprise has two facets–the entrepreneurs and enterprise. The person, who takes the risk of venture creation and the subsequent management, is the entrepreneur. A viable opportunity, identified and launched, as a project becomes the enterprise. The entrepreneur could be a single person or a group of persons.

These are the persons who not only dream about their ventures, but also know how to dream. They are the people with vision and leadership, backed by their achievement motivation and drive to succeed.

The growth of the enterprise depends on several factors. These are dependent on the socio-economic background and motivational factors behind the enterprise. In small enterprises, often it is difficult to separate the entrepreneur who is owner–manager from the enterprise. The entrepreneur and the enterprise, by and large, form a shadow of each other. The owner-managers shoulder the responsibility for all the daily routine operations, as well as the planning for growth or expansion.

SMALL ENTERPRISES

To appreciate the growth and development of entrepreneurship, a basic understanding of the definition and scope of the terminology "small enterprise" is very necessary. The definition of a small enterprise varies across countries, industries, agencies and authors. The terminology "small enterprise" itself is used by different countries by different nomenclatures such as small business, small firm and small industries and so on. Throughout

Table 1
Terminologies and Scope of Small Industry in Select Countries

Country	*Terminology*	*Scope*
Japan	Small enterprise	Manufacturing, mining, services, trading (wholesale and retail)
India	Small Industry/ Small enterprise	Manufacturing, repair and servicing.
Korea	Small enterprise	Manufacturing, mines, construction, commerce.
USA/Canada	Small Business	Manufacturing, services, trading (Limited)
UK	Small Firms	Manufacturing, Commerce (both retail and wholesale) construction, mining, transport.
Indonesia	Small Industry	Manufacturing, servicing.

this study the terms small enterprise, small firm and small business are used interchangeably. Vepa[1] has listed the various terminologies used in some countries are presented in Table 1.

Atkins and Lowe[2] noted that as many as 40 different definitions of small firms have been reported in the literature, and generally there appears to be very little consistency in criteria used to define small enterprises. The criteria are many, such as number of employees, annual sales revenue, value of fixed assets/plant and machinery and the management structure.

In India, the small industry is defined in terms of investment ceiling. Also the small industry sector enjoys a special reservation policy in terms of items of manufacture. The investment limit ceiling was revised by the central government from time to time, depending on the industrial and economic development and needs of entrepreneurs. The evolution of investment limits of small industries in India is shown in Table 2

Table 2

Evolution of Investment Limit for Small Industries

Year	*Investment*	*Additional Condition*
1950	Up to Rs. 0.5 million in fixed assets	Less than 50 employees with power or 100 employees without power.
1960	Up to Rs. 0.5 million in fixed assets	No condition
1966	Up to Rs. 0.75million in plant & machinery	No condition
1975	Up to Rs. 1million in plant & machinery	No condition
1980	Up to Rs. 2million in plant & machinery	No condition
1985	Up to Rs. 3.5 million in plant & machinery	No condition
1991	Up to Rs. 6 million in plant & machinery	No condition
1997	Up to Rs. 30 million in plant & machinery	No condition
1999	Up to Rs. 10 million in plant & machinery	No condition

Initially, there was an additional condition limiting number of persons employed, the same was deleted in 1960. Further, the investment ceiling was linked to plant and machinery only, excluding investment in other fixed assets i.e., land and building. The reason was to define small industry with respect to such investments mainly in productive assets.

The investment limit was raised to Rs. 30 million based on the recommendations of the Report of the Expert Committee on Small Enterprises, with Dr. Abid Hossain as Chairman. The report, submitted to the Central Government in July 1997, recommended that the definition of small scale industries be broadened to small scale enterprises and allowing incentives, credit facilities, and promotional facilities to flow to all small enterprises. On line with this, it was recommended that the investment limit of small scale enterprise be raised to Rs. 30 million. But later, it was felt that this raise in investment limit up to Rs. 30 million did not truly result in accelerated investments in small enterprises. Large majority of small enterprises still belong to the lower investments up to Rs. 1million . There was also an apprehension that with the increased investment limit up to Rs. 30 million , some of the medium scale may roll back to small scale thus bringing in unhealthy competition. Therefore, the investment ceiling was, for the first time in 1999, reduced from Rs. 30 million to Rs. 10 million.

It was in 1977, the Central Government introduced a new category namely "Tiny Sector Industries" with the small scale industry category, particularly to provide promotional measures and incentives to such of the small industries having much lower investment limits. The present investment limit for tiny sector industries is Rs. 2.5 million in plant and machinery. For the purpose of this study, the tiny sector is also considered as part of small enterprises.

In United States, the Small Business Administration, established in 1953, provided financial, technical and management assistance to help Americans to start, run and grow their businesses. The size standards of Small Business Administration define whether a business entity is small; and thus eligible for government assistance reserved for small business concerns. Small

Business Administration establishes size standards considering economic characteristics, comprising the structure of industry, including degree of competition, average firm size, start-up costs and entry barrier and distribution of firm by size. It also considers technological change, competition from other industries, growth trends, and historical activity within an industry. As reported in homepage of Small Business Administration, America's 25 million small businesses employ more than 50 percent of the private workforce, generate more than half of the nation's gross domestic product, and are the principal source of new jobs in the US economy.

Bolton Committee Report in UK indicates that a small firm is defined by the number of persons employed, (less than 200 for manufacturing, less than 25 for construction and less than 5 vehicles for transport) and by turnover for retail trade (less than turnover £50,000) and wholesale trade (less than turnover of £200,000).

According to European Union[3] approach the businesses are classified as micro firms (less than 10 people) ; small firms (10–49 employees) ; and medium–sized firms (50–249 employees). Frequently, researchers combine small and medium firms into a single category i.e., small and medium-size enterprises. Those with 250 or more employees are classified as the large firms.

Besides the statistical definition of small enterprises in different countries, Atkins and Lowe argue that the structure and decision making process of an organization should be the primary indicator of a small firm. They explain that statistical definition of smallness such as number of employees or annual receipts may omit significant dimensions of small firms. They refer to the involvement of the business owners in the strategic planning, forecasting, and performance comparison of small firms. Further, Resnik[4] argues that one of the defining criteria of small firms is the involvement of the owner-manager in setting the business priorities, objectives, and standards. This argument suggests that a firm may be classified as small, based upon the role of the owner-managers and the extent to which their direct participation in the management of the business.

Alternatively, the small enterprises can be defined using qualitative approach. Bolton Committee Report in UK provided one of the best-known approaches. This was in the form of an ideal type combining three elements.

First, in economic terms, a small firm is one that has a relatively small share of market. Secondly, an essential characteristic of a small firm is that its owners or part-owners manage it in a personalized way, and not through the medium of formalized management structure. Thirdly, it is also independent in the sense that it does not form part of a larger enterprise and that the owner-managers should be free from outside control in taking their principal decisions[5].

Haksever[6] notes that "in case of small firms, the management is independent; usually the owner is one of the managers and reports to no one". The summary of Haksever incorporates the guidelines established by the US Small Business Administration, (Guide to SBA: Definitions of Small Business, 1996) and arguments of Atkins and Lowe. Haksever defines a small business as one with fewer than 500 employees and exemplifying the following characteristics:

1. Management is independent; usually the manager is also owner.
2. Capital is supplied and ownership is held by an individual or a small group.
3. The area of operations is mainly local; workers and owners tend to be in one home community, although markets need not be.
4. The business is small, compared to the biggest units in the field.

Nolan used the above definition in his doctoral research on small business performance. In Indian context, Chachadi[7] also adopted similar definition in his doctoral research work on

'Decision Making in Small Industry', as it incorporates managerial aspects like ownership and control. The definition of Government of India only refers to ceiling on investment in plant and machinery, which relates to economic aspects, because financial and capital resources of small enterprises are not so abundant, as in developed countries. The definition of Haksever has added significance to the present study, as it does not ignore local area of operation and local owners and employees.

In an attempt to formulate qualitative definitions of small firms, a key assumption made, was that small firms were fundamentally different from large firms. In one of the classics of small business theorizing[8] this assumption was summed up in the analogy that small and large firms were fundamentally different from each other as caterpillars are from butterflies. It was noted that even if one metamorphosis into other, it would not be simply larger version of the other, and in case of small firms, the chance of metamorphosis is also not certain. Many small firms may never grow beyond a small size, as most of the 'caterpillars' may never become butterflies[9].

Regarding size, Burrows and Curran[10] argue as " Size, whether measured in terms of number of employees, turnover, market share whatever, is not sufficiently robust criterion to allow 'small firms' to be isolated and analyzed as having an economic and social specificity". These authors continue their arguments that smallness per *se is* not technically a necessary characteristic of an organization but a *contingent* one. Smallness has the same status as other characteristics such as legal form of organization, type of economic activity engaged, the technology employed, region or local economy, the age, gender, ethnicity and educational level of the owners or workers of the firm etc.

Phansalkar[11], a consultant to small industries in India, argues that there is no firm, indisputable and yet defensible criterion for delimiting terms such as small or large industry. What in India considered being a giant, say automobile manufacturing companies, may be possibly small in the eyes of a global player in auto industry.

He further states that, in Indian situation, basis of categorization on sales turnover, or investment in fixed assets could also pose problems, because there are instances of one-man-show in an oil mill, where the sales turnover could be over Rs.1500 lakhs (150 Million). Small enterprises may employ a few people, and the management levels may be of simple structure. On the other hand, small enterprises having low capital investment, according to the statistical definition, could be involved in complex business. In his opinion, the only possible and defensible ground for categorization of small, medium and large industry in Indian context is by differentiating their management problems. This means that amount of complexity involved in management of enterprises becomes a key parameter for differentiating enterprises as small or large. Parameters such as sales turnover, investment in fixed assets, or number of employees are simply surrogates for complexity. Therefore, the paradox that by definition, the small enterprises management ought to be simpler, but seldom it is.

Based on the above arguments on defining the small enterprises, it would be unrealistic to demand uniformity of approach in small business research. While the European Union definition of micro and small firms is widely used, many researchers used the combination of definitions framed by Small Business Administration[12], Atkins and Lowe[13] and Hoksever[14].

ENTREPRENEURSHIP AND ENTREPRENEURIAL STUDIES IN ABROAD

A.P Alexander[15] has conducted a study of 354 Greek Industrialists, pertaining to the supply of entrepreneurs and the nature of their policies. He observed that "the reforms of kemal Ataturk inflicted damage to the prestige and status of some groups of Greek people. These groups were well attracted by the lure of large profits and new opportunities". He identifies the following as some of the root causes for the low success rate of Greek entrepreneurs, high cost of production, inability to tackle problems effectively, and unsympathetic attitude towards workers, reluctance to share with others ownership and control of enterprise influence of Greek cultural values and lack of proper educational base for their role as managers. Alexander also noticed that there was considerable upward mobility in entrepreneurial activity among those whom he studied.

John Harris[16] has conducted a study of 269 Nigerian entrepreneurs, engaged in different industrial activities like saw milling, manufacturing of furniture, printing, rubber processing, garment making and banking. Harris finds that the Nigerian entrepreneurs are almost successful in identifying opportunities and gaining command over resources, but they are relatively unsuccessful in the management of enterprises. Harris[17] has listed some of the factors hindering entrepreneurial development in Africa, as identified by some other too: difference between the social world in which as African entrepreneur lives and economic world in which he has to operate[18], undeveloped and uninstitutional way of gaining knowledge, recruiting skills and borrowing money; lack of interregional mobility, lack of commercial experience, oligopolistic market conditions[19], shortage of viable projects[20], absence of business eniviroment[21] and management deficiency resulting in low level of capacity utilization, lack of prudent financial management and little propensity to innovate[22]

Peter Kilby[23] observes that in Lagos, another African county, socio cultural factors hinder the development of entrepreneurial characteristics. According to Peter Maris[24] African entrepreneurs have been able to reach great heights because of their ability to separate domestic matters from business matters. Development of contracts, widening the horizon of experience and breaking the vicious circle of isolation can foster entrepreneurship in African countries which can struggle to develop.

Yousif A.Sayigh[25] studied in 1956 207 Lebanese entrepreneurs engaged in manufacturing, agriculture, financial and service sectors. In Lebanon, Christians constituted a disproportionate share of innovating entrepreneurs. The major occupation of the entrepreneurs prior to their present activity was trade which together with industry comprised about two thirds of their previous occupations. They viewed their own economic and social statuses as higher than those of their fathers. In subsequent analysis of the Arab world made in the sixties, Saysigh stressed that through cultural values did pose some resistance to development, they were not as strong as they are believed to be by the sociologists.

Hoselitz's study of the French and British entrepreneurs gave prime importance to capital formation and work experiences, among factors influencing entrepreneurship among them[26]. The French entrepreneurs are conservative, security-minded, valuing independence to preference to growth, cautious, thrifty and calvinist.

With reference to Indonesia, which had been under the occupation of the Dutch, Higgins notes that entrepreneurship developed on the Indonesian Islands where the impact of Dutch destruction has entrepreneurial motives was not deep rooted. While Balians have a group's focused image of change, the Japanese have also focused image of change[27].

In another study of Indonesian entrepreneurs, Kroef[28] considered the entrepreneurs in relation to the middle class of the country. He emphasized that the economic development of the country was impeded by political factors and he did not consider the religious or cultural factors as impediments to the entrepreneurial development in Indonesia.

Carroll[29] in his survey of 92 industrial entrepreneurship in the Philippines, a development economy identified the causes for the entrepreneurs originating disproportionately from big cities. He also found that their culture contributed to entrepreneurial success. Further, he observed that there was a very impressive amount of mobility in the family of the entrepreneurs.

Gustav Papanek[30] conducted in 1959 a survey of 250 industrialists in Pakistan, each employing twenty or more workers. With the partition of the former United India and the dominant Hindu Businessman leaving the country, all opportunities for development in Pakistan remained exclusively with the Muslim business community. Papanek identified that economic incentives, conditions of acute scarcity in the country, contraction of foreign trade, import of machinery at liberalization terms, contributed significantly to develop and encourage a good number of industrial entrepreneurs, he argues that the findings of his study lend support to the view that entrepreneurship in manufacturing arose in response to powerful economic incentives rather than significant changes in socio-psychological variables. Further, he maintained that responsive bureaucracy, favourable government policies, a value system and institutional not hostile to entrepreneurship, a group of responsive traders and a stable political system contributed in favour of the growth and development of entrepreneurship.

Susumu Watanabe[31] found that in Japan, as in other countries, small entrepreneurs have to overcome various barriers in order to set up business. Competition appears to be much fiercer than in developing countries. In a sense, therefore the difficulties and risks are greater. A majority of entrepreneurs spend more than ten years, preparing for their venture, often working in the evenings after their regular day time employment. A combination of strong will power, thriftiness, hard work and ambition produced the abundant supply of Entrepreneurship in Japanese manufacturing.

Sharma[32] conducted a comparative study of the promotion of small enterprises by institutions and agencies in the developing countries of Asia, such as Malaysia, Bangladesh, Thailand, Korea, Hong Kong, India and Philippines. This study identified that the policy for the promotion of small industries in all these countries was defective, as it suffered from a lack of integration, organization and exclusiveness. In some cases, the policies of formulations were not clear and they needed constant revision. Sharma found hardly any co-ordination among the various support organizations to evolve an appropriate and integrated approach.

Battacharya[33] studied the industrial and agricultural entrepreneurs of eleven South East Asian counties namely Brunei, Cambodia, Indonesia, India, Laos, Malaysia, North Vietnam,

Singapore, South Vietnam, Philippines and Thailand. He evolved a model of entrepreneurial development for these countries based on his indepth study of the problems and prospects of entrepreneurs. However, he felt that the model by itself would not work miracles, unless sustained Herculean efforts were made to solve the complex and deep rooted problems in each country.

In another study and entrepreneurship in Pakistan Zafar Altaf[34] found that decentralized management practices, dispersal of location of family support, competitive spirit and change in motives from profit to patriotism and independence were responsible for the success of the entrepreneurs. He also noticed that education was a modernizing factor of Pakistani entrepreneurs and that occupational representation in entrepreneurship was growing.

Peter F. Drucker[35] in "Innovation and Entrepreneurship-practice and principles" discussed at length the sources for innovative opportunity. He classified such sources into two types, such as sources lying within the industry (the unexpected, the incongruity, the process need, and the changes in the industry structure) and sources outside the industry (Demographics, changes in perception, and the new knowledge).

M.M.P. Akhouri[36] while examining the policies, programme and progress made by small scale industries in ten Asian countries, highlighted the concept of integrated entrepreneurship development and its close linkages to the Small Scale Industries development. The author made a comparative study of the stimulatory, supporting and sustaining activities of entrepreneurship development in seven Asian countries. The policy implementation gaps in entrepreneurship development were highlighted with empirical evidence.

Umesh C. Patnaik[37] reported that in Canada, the ideas of business and Entrepreneurship are instilled even in the minds of Kids of Kindergarten. The author remarked "Entrepreneurship education for development of small scale business in Canada had become a matter of academic interest since long and that business culture is largely shaped in Canadian class room".

Sukhal Singh[38] in his study of refugees from Pakistan as entrepreneurs found that the factors influencing the success of entrepreneurs are determination to adjust in new environment, previous experience and knowledge and the measures adopted by government to facilitate rehabilitation. He suggested that not only family background; personal motivation and conducive environment but also Government policies and programmes will promote entrepreneurship.

Cas Feng Qi [39] underlines that entrepreneurs are not necessarily business owners because the evolution of the modern corporate system has gradually resulted in the separation of ownership and management. He further emphasizes that an effective motivation system is very much necessary for the entrepreneurs to improve productivity.

Tyler[40] conducted a comparative study on the supply of goods and services on Entrepreneurship and Small Business (ESB) to the demands of customers. The investigations produced a description of the mismatch of demands for goods and services to the supply of goods and services, benchmark of business activities for starting businesses, list of exemplary ESB books and checklist of product evaluation attributes. Finally, he recommended a model for Entrepreneurship, job description, curricula and model for a cash flow business plan analysis audit.

Bolika[41] has conducted a study in Japan, Zaire and Thailand countries with different historical, cultural and economic backgrounds on Human Resource Management practices can make improvements of market share and profit among small and medium enterprises. He identified that successful small and medium enterprise entrepreneurs are those who trust their employees, give them training, and seek employee participation in the decision-making process. He also recommended that entrepreneurs of small and medium enterprises should concentrate on Human Resource Management variables, rather than entrepreneurial path, finance, technology and environment. His findings clearly establish that Human Resource Management is the most critical function to the productivity of small and medium enterprises.

Fangs[42] study investigates the social organization of entrepreneurship and the emergence of markets by interviewing with business owners and government officials in China. He found that the growth of private firms in China as a response to market incentives, which is a result of the gradual retreat of the state's monopoly over resource allocation; 'path dependent' nature of economic reform also creates opportunities to entrepreneurs into certain market niches; existing system of stratification blocks forcing some individuals to look for alternatives in the emerging market sector and finally state itself protecting and regulating business behaviour.

Omoiele[43] conducted a study to examine the perception of 16 selected African American entrepreneurs who had experienced success or failure and found socio-cultural and socio- opportunistic is responsible for their success or failure. In the same study, he surveyed the opinion of 148 African American Consumers on African American businesses failure/success. He noticed that traditional African American businesses got success as they are located in or out of ethnic enclaves where as non-traditional businesses had failed due to the lack of patronage of African American Consumers.

Heidman[44] conducted a study to identify key aspects of midlife executive women's perceptions of their transition into new ways of self employed work. It is about learning, change and growth. He identified autonomy, financial security, women's values, better balance and an improved quality of life is responsible for such transition and growth.

Charles[45] conducted a study to analyze the two approaches of economic theory from the perspective of modern Austrian economies particularly Israel Kirzners's theory of entrepreneurship. In the course of his study, questions are addressed concerning entrepreneurial error, increasing returns, technologies and persuasiveness as an alternative to entrepreneurial discovery. He finds an analytical distinction is drawn between the private domain and public domain which allows the effects of entrepreneurship within and outside of the market constraint to be contrasted. It is seen that growth – promoting entrepreneurship is dependent upon a particular structure of property rights and supporting institutions, in order to be able to build complex structure of capital which permit growth.

Bellard[46] has conducted a study to establish the potential role of the entrepreneur in reconstructing the modern Russian economy. He observed different schools of thought regarding the roles and importance of the entrepreneur in a non-static capitalist economy. The history of entrepreneurship in Imperial Russia is then examined, followed by a documentation of the efforts of entrepreneurs under the socialist system. Finally, he concluded that the work is non-ethnocentric in its analysis.

Selameab[47] has conducted a study of 315 entrepreneurial trainers of Minneapolis St. Paul based Technical and Community colleges between 1989-93 inclusive to identify uncovering new insights into the relationships between education and entrepreneurship, by examining the business start-up experiences of completers of entrepreneurial trainings. Second, to identify factors in the investment environment that may have enhances or hampered business start-ups. He concluded that the continued offering of entrepreneurship training programme in the Twin cities to enhance new venture formations is warranted. Environmental constraints for starting business in the region were not perceived detrimental. Training components such as business plans, finance, marketing and projects appeared to be influential for business start-ups.

Mitra D.K, Bhatia.G.S, Pannuselvam.R and Marytt Powel [48] have indicated that there is need for entrepreneurial training so as to promote the entrepreneurship in order to solve the problems of unemployment. They have emphasized the need for carrying out research continuously so as to evolve the entrepreneurial development models with appropriate training methods.

Mark Cassan[49] considered that the managerial skills and leadership are the prime factors, and financial skill and risk bearing are the secondary factors, that promote the entrepreneurial development. He has observed that strong desire to make profit and liquidity of wealth, will act as instruments in making the industrial entrepreneurs as successful Entrepreneurs.

Richard[50] in his paper, compared and contrasted financial profiles for a longitudinal panel of 871 small and medium-sized enterprises(SMEs) in the Australian manufacturing sector that have embarked upon different development pathways and to examine possible connections between enterprise growth and the experience of common financial problems. Collectively, the findings represent a departure from much received knowledge in SME financial scholarship. The experience of growth seems not to have influenced the return on investment, asset structure, financial structure, liquidity and solvency ratios studies; but the margin, operating expenses, turnover and financing expense ratios do appear to be affected by growth. Over all, the financial profiles produced are quite remarkable; there is no evidence of problematic financial consequences of growth. The only differences in financial profiles found, are those that are readily explained by differences in the scale or growth resource needs of the business examined.

Benson[51] conducted a study on 64 small manufacturing businesses that have undergone or were experiencing radical political and economic upheaval in the West Bank town of Ramallah in the Paleslinian Territories. The findings of this research were preliminary and requiring further confirmation should provide helpful insights into strategies of assisting and insulating other small businesses that have experienced major environmental upheavals. In particular, the study challenges commonly held assumptions regarding the importance of business experience, formal education, and of plant capital, highlighting the need to asses comparatively the heterogeneity of the small and medium sized enterprises(SMEs). It suggests that successful interventions will require additional research in the areas of organizational expertise and technological capabilities of SMEs in such environments.

Huang, Xueli, Soutar, Geoffrey and Alan[52] examined the New Product Development Process (NPDP) in 276 innovative Australian Small and Medium-Sized Enterprises (SMEs). Findings suggested that marketing - related activities were undertaken less frequently and were less well executed than technical activities in developing new products. However, marketing-related activities were important in distinguishing between successful and unsuccessful new products. In addition, resource and skill availability and new product planning were positively associated with the quality with which NPD activities are executed. Further, the existence of a new product strategy seemed to have a significant positive impact on the quality of NPD activities.

Lebrasseur, Zanibbi and Zinger[53] examined the relationships between pre-start-up activities, expansion intention and expansion activities and how these combine to influence early stage performance from 145 new ventures across the north-eastern Ontario. The study suggests that at the early start-up, the entrepreneur needs to resist the temptation to become immersed in day-to-day operating issues and turn attention to building a base of managerial capabilities that will enable the growing firm to meet to the demands of the market place.

Subrahmanya[54] conducted a comparative study in 34 small engineering enterprises probing the nature and dimensions of technological innovations carried out in north-east England and in the Bangalore urban district. Technological innovations of small enterprises may take different forms depending upon various factors, internal as well as external to an enterprise. But the casual factors, sources and dimensions of technological innovations, radical and incremental, in small engineering enterprises appear to be similar between these two regions.

Ayala, Dov and Sadeh[55] conducted an exploratory study with 25 Israeli high-technology entrepreneurs, focusing on their personal as well as professional backgrounds. Results reveal that the high technical education, a technical profession and a small family tended to be successful Israeli entrepreneurs. It also finds that most of the entrepreneurs are coming from ethnic and religious minority groups with fathers who were self-employed and an involved family that supported early start-up activities.

Mitchell [56] examined the motivation of entrepreneurs in starting a business in the socio-economic milieu of 101 male and female entrepreneurs of South Africa. It also aims to identify similarities and differences in the motive profiles of these male and female entrepreneurs. The results were that both men and women entrepreneurs were found to be primarily motivated by the need for independence, need for material incentives and the need for achievement. Male entrepreneurs in comparison to females were more motivated by the need to provide family security and to make a difference in the business. Female entrepreneurs more than males were motivated by the need to keep learning and the need for more money to survive.

ENTREPRENEURSHIP AND ENTREPRENEURIAL STUDIES IN INDIA

In the early fifties Mc Crory[57] studied small scale firms, 14 in chopur and 3 in Moradabad towns in Uttar Pradesh with the objective of finding out whether there were typical patterns of growth in the small machine industries and if so, to isolate, by comparing the case histories of individual enterprise , the common factors that were associated with growth, decline or stagnation. He considered family background in crafts as a necessary source of good industrial entrepreneurs. He analyzed the causes for the high mortality rate among the firms and lack of growth in them. He recommended that an opportunity to grow be given to them through provision of capital.

Gadgil[58] in his historical study of India's industrial evolution, observed that the economic development of the country was mangled by the Colonial rule; otherwise the craft based industries had been flourishing well at the beginning of the eighteenth century. He[59] also listed the communities involved in trade, finance and handicrafts industries in the different geographical regions of India during the seventeenth and eighteenth centuries.

Adrew Brimmer[60] conducted an intensive and analytical study of the managing agency system on the setting of entrepreneurship in India. In his study, he explains the origin and growth of the system and indicated its contributions to economic development. He argues that the managing agency system of industrial organization was the result of efforts by the British and Indian entrepreneurs to overcome the hardships caused by the lack of capital and business acumen. This system gave more scope for such scarce factors as finance and management but it led to extensive concentration of wealth in a few and malpractices.

Berna[61] conducted an indepth study of 52 medium scale manufacturing units engaged in light engineering production in and around the Madras and Coimbatore cities. His study purports to review the occupational and socio economic background of the group of entrepreneurs, their origin, the way in which they became entrepreneurs, and the hardships they faced in the establishment and development of their enterprises. This study reveals that 85% of the enterprises established as small scale units, were developed over the years into medium scale units. He observed that many entrepreneurs have been diversifying production activity and shifting it into new lines of activity, but their performance in technological improvement has not been impressive. Dr. Berna feels that if a certain package of help in techniques of production process and management could be provided to the entrepreneurs, their performance could be considerably improved.

The UNESCO Research Centre[62] in its study on a metal industry of Howrah in West Bengal observed that the industrial entrepreneurship sprang up gradually owing to a shift in the entrepreneurs from their traditional occupation to industry. This might have been due to their educational attainment, which stimulated prospective entrepreneurs to come out with a resolve to succeed.

Rao and Sumithra[63] identified some of the factors, which stimulated and others, which impeded the growth of entrepreneurship. They made an attempt to study the role of government policies and programmes in promoting entrepreneurship. They felt that, though the policies of the government in some cases failed entrepreneurship, they played a positive role in most cases. They assessed this role in terms of the abilities of the entrepreneurs to increase their assets, to diversify their products and to widen their market.

Hazlehurst[64] studied Ramnagar (a fictitious name for a town on India & Pakistan Border) entrepreneurs and examined the impact of migration on the entrepreneurial structure and observed that the entrepreneurial continuity was augmented by the migrant entrepreneurs and also that the refugee entrepreneurs proved to be more innovative than the local entrepreneurs.

Amlendu Guha[65] reviewed in his articles, the growth of the Parsi business community, in particular in its transitional phase, over a period of 100 years till 1850. He held that religion Puritanism could not be considered as wholly responsible for the success of the Parsi entrepreneurs. He believed that neither religion nor Puritanism explains the achievement orientation of the Parsis. Their interest in European forms of business organizations, exploration of new markets, business acumen and acquisition of a working knowledge of the English language are major contributory factors to their commendable success in business and industry.

Subramanian, Shivakumar and Palanisomi[66] conducted a modest survey of 150 small entrepreneurs in the Madurai city and its environs, with a view to delineating the characteristics of entrepreneurs in small scale industries in a particular locality of

Madurai and its environs and the influential factors of entrepreneurship.

Ashis Nandy and Raymond L. Owvens[67] analyzed on exploratory basis, some of the psychological and social correlates of entrepreneurship in an urban community of Howrah (West Bengal) and compared two caste groups within the community. This was an attempt to compare the enterprising and non-enterprising cultures.

Paul A. London's[68] study, is an unusual study, because it focuses on rural merchants, a lively and enterprising group rarely mentioned in development literature. The study, based on nearly 200 interviews, shows that little noticed, often abused private shopkeepers adapted remarkably to India's rural needs in the past decade by selling hundreds of millions of dollars worth of vital fertilizers and irrigation equipment. Their work helped make agricultural gains possible yet the Indian Government barely tolerates their continued existence in rural areas.

Three Scholars Moulik, Patel & Basu[69] made a study of 100 non-agricultural entrepreneurs drawn from a dozen villages of the Anand Taluka in Gujarat. They grouped these entrepreneurs under three broad categories of manufacturing, processing and trade or services, and found that the entrepreneurs of these groups needed three different sets of traits for their success.

R.A.Sharma[70] conducted a study to evaluate the performance of promoters of 316 non- government manufacturing companies, which were incorporated on or after April 1, 1947 in terms of entrepreneurial growth after Independence. The study identified and explained in detail the environmental factors affecting entrepreneurship institutional finance and other resources of the entrepreneurs and vocational mobility of entrepreneurs.

Entrepreneurship is also conditioned by political forces and administrative system and its commitment to economic development was pointed out by Manohar U. Deshpande[71]. The study also mentioned that the upper state of the society enjoyed most of the benefits created by governmental agencies, and such they enjoyed a better socio–economic position in the society.

Singh.P.N's[72] study based on some cases of successful entrepreneurs aims at identifying factors for success and for development entrepreneurship for economic growth in a country. He examined the social values related to the importance of entrepreneurship in economic development, governmental efforts to encourage entrepreneurs and the factors influencing entrepreneurship and suggest a model for entrepreneurial development.

Hadimani[73] conducted a survey of 200 traditionally trading entrepreneurs belonging to the weaving and non-weaving castes, in the handloom industry of Mahantapur. His study indicated the attachment to the caste occupation was strong, but interestingly it promoted entrepreneurship in the case of the trading caste and hindered it in the case of the weaving caste. He is of the view that, this dual role of caste entrepreneurship is mainly due to the presence or lack of several social, economic, political , educational and human resources factors.

Gupta[74] recently studied entrepreneurial performances of 60 small entrepreneurs, taking 20 each from Kanpur, Allahabad & Garakhpur in Uttar Pradesh. In his study he deals in detail with the essential qualities and functions of entrepreneurs, policy framework and support systems to develop entrepreneurship in the small sector. He made recommendations for framing policies in future and outlines the role of the government in developing entrepreneurship in the small industry sector.

Bhanusahli[75] had made a study of 125 light engineering industries of Kolhapur in the Maharastra State, with particular reference to the economic, social, educational and occupational backgrounds of the entrepreneurs. He has also examined the organizational set up, personnel production, finance, marketing and entrepreneurial creation on the basis of which the development of entrepreneur's personality is charted. He concluded that persons from the minority or marginal groups trained in the art of engineering and having long contact with engineering industry have better capabilities to achieve success.

Patel.V.G[76] under a World Bank Research Project studied the three Gujarat innovations, (1) The Technicians and New Entrepreneurs Scheme of Finance (TSNES), (2) Entrepreneurship Development Programme (EDP) and (3) The sheds construction Programme for Industrial Infrastructure, to assess the effectiveness of such innovative policies and programmes on new entrepreneurship formation. It was concluded that (i) Programmes are effective in accelerating the development of small scale industries; (ii) Potential industrial entrepreneurship is lying latent in a variety of Castes, communities and occupational groups; (iii) Success in the venture is the result of enterprise and competence rather than financial position of the entrepreneur; and (iv) EDPs can address those with inadequate entrepreneurial and managerial capacities and individual information and self confidence.

Khanka[77] studied 50 small scale entrepreneurs in a notified backward region of the Kumaun division of Uttar Pradesh regarding the emergence, performance and problems of entrepreneurship. A guiding assumption of this study is that true display of the entrepreneurial role and attributes can be well seen only in the case of small scale entrepreneurs. The study brought under its purview entrepreneurship setting entry into entrepreneurship, financing of entrepreneurship, entrepreneurial performance and their problems. Khanka laid stress on the policy implications to provide liberal incentives and concessions to the entrepreneurs to encourage, promote and strengthen the small units in backward areas.

Venkatachalam and Saleendran[78] had given a conceptual frame work and importance of innovation in their paper entitled "Innovation and Entrepreneurship". According to them, innovators have an undying need to make inroads into something new which others will take years to attempt, the product being technologically or geographically new. The innovations that an entrepreneur is expected to carry out are: Introduction of new goods, new methods of production, creating new markets, finding new sources of raw materials or manufactured goods and building a new organization as of many industries.

Personality study of successful and unsuccessful entrepreneurs was conducted by Tahera Mashauddin[79]. An interesting finding of the study is that most of the unsuccessful entrepreneurs reported a steep fall from initial high level of expectations (8.4) to the present level of expectations (4.1). This perhaps is due to the fact that while most of the successful entrepreneurs tend to make a realistic estimate of their future expectations based on their present experiences, the unsuccessful entrepreneurs apparently do not do so. Personality is an important factor besides economic insight and managerial efficiency in influencing entrepreneurial success.

Bisht and Sharma[80] have studied the entrepreneurial planning and setting by surveying 150 entrepreneurs of the Faridabad District in Harayana. Their study entails a wide spectrum of carefully planned investigative entrepreneurial dimensions involving entrepreneurial setting and some empirical evidences. The investigators found that the modern setting the caste factor is not as important as the family factor, and that the inter-generational/intra generational influences are the dominant factors deciding the course of entrepreneurial history and its repetitive nature. An important findings of the study is that majority of the entrepreneurs surveyed have hardly any business or traditional background.

Small industry is considered to promote entrepreneurship. As Louks[81] observed, throughout the 1960s, and 1980s there has been a growing awareness of the small business sector and the importance of entrepreneurship to the growth of the economy. This has been true in both the developed and developing economics of the world.

Ashis Gupta[82] studied Indian entrepreneurial culture by interviewing more than ninety prominent Indian business owners, owner-managers and managers of whom some were first and others second or third generation, some trained in business and engineering schools, while a few had no formal training. His contention was that it was far from certain that cultural and religious influences give rise to an aspect of entrepreneurial behaviour and what is certain is the diversity of background, motives and strategies that run through the nature of entrepreneurship.

Ajit Kanitkar[83] advocated the adoption of 'Extension approach' by the support systems. A number of reasons were listed for the low success rate of entrepreneurship training programmes. The prominent among which was the unsympathetic and often hostile response of the support system. Based on the experience of organizing two extension motivation programmes in the North Eastern-States of India, he concluded that human component of the support system had to be sensitized to influence the external environment.

Chandra[84] reported that significant differences could be found between successful and unsuccessful entrepreneurs when risk taking was considered along with other factors.

Vinayshil Gautham[85] discussed the concept and constraints of science and technology entrepreneurship. He advocated the need to develop an entrepreneurship index, a measure of individual's strengths and weaknesses to make entrepreneurship development a more selective, intensive and purposive process rather than that of a mass application.

Ravi K. Zutshi[86] discussed the need to mould entrepreneurs who are better equipped to create hi-tech enterprises. In order to nurture entrepreneurship among persons with science and technical education, the author suggested a programme package consisting of entrepreneurial awareness, skill development, prototype design, project work, confidence building etc.,

Kamla Singh[87] conducted a study in three districts namely Faridabad, Gurgaon and Hisar, in the state of Haryana. A total of 64 Women Entrepreneurs who were engaged in production of goods/services of trade activities were covered under the sample of the study. It focused mainly on the linkages and communication pattern between women entrepreneurs and their supporting agencies. It also provided a profile of these Women Entrepreneurs, motivation, entrepreneurial traits and the study indicated that better efficient linkages and better communication between the entrepreneurs and supporting agencies enhance entrepreneurial performance and success and constraints. It is interesting to note that the study as a part of its conclusions, mentions that knowledge, entrepreneurial motivation and 'entrepreneurial profit' contribute significantly and positively towards improving performance of entrepreneurs.

Jawahar.R.M.P[88] studied nine Science and Technology Entrepreneurship Development Programmes conducted by the Science Park and concluded: (1) Higher the educational qualification lesser the possibility of taking up entrepreneur career; (2) Persons in the age group of 25 and less showed highest success rate; (3) 80 percent of the units were below the investment level of Rs.1million and; (4) 60 percent of the units were engaged in consumer goods production.

A study on Women Entrepreneurs was carried out by M. Sargad-haran and R.Beegam[89]. It was a survey conducted on 415 Women Entrepreneurs in Kerala, who were engaged in a variety of business enterprises. The survey presents the socio-economic profile, nature of enterprise and information about the Governmental and Non-Governmental institutional support.

Ahluwalia[90] mentioned the importance of industrialization as a means of achieving rapid growth and prosperity has all along been recognized in the thinking on development strategy for Independent India.

Prabath, S.V[91] has opined that, there is need to review the Entrepreneurship Development Programme in the context of globalization and the new economic policy so as to strengthen the Entrepreneurship Development Programme in order to develop the prospective entrepreneurs.

Lillian Vernonkatz[92] has identified that, the need for achievement, risk taking, role models, locus of control are the key elements in entrepreneurial motivation. He has stressed the need for entrepreneurial education in the area of finance, strategic planning, marketing and management, for promoting the entrepreneurial development.

Chandra Poojary, M[93] has observed that, the motivational factors, personality attributes and functions of the entrepreneurs vary considerably, and depend on the prevailing socio-economic conditions and other factors.

Ranjeeth Asthana, K[94] has indicated that there is need for adopting the Entrepreneurship Development Programme in order to provide the latent talent to the entrepreneurs so as to take the advantage of the growth opportunities. He has stressed that greater cooperation among the agencies involved in providing Entrepreneurship Development Programme is necessary so as to train the entrepreneurs efficiently.

Shallappan, R., and Venkatapathy, R.,[95] have observed that the developed countries are achieving higher growth rates owing to the entrepreneurial activity. They have recommended that the government has to make efforts to formulate and adopt better schemes to develop the potential entrepreneurs, with the entrepreneurial talents. They have advocated that there is need to bridge the gap between entrepreneurial awareness and practices.

Anitha, H.S and Laxmishra, A.S[96] analyzed that the emergence of Women Entrepreneurs, depends on the economic, social, psychological and cultural and other factors. They have stressed that, the provision of entrepreneurial education, financing and marketing facilities and the adoption of promotional measures and policies by the governmental and non-governmental agencies would promote the women-entrepreneurship development.

A study was conducted by A.S.Vasudev Rao[97] in Dakshina Kannada district of Karnataka, to understand the problems and prospects of small enterprise consultancy, attitudes and determinants of consultancy and its impact on enterprise performance. The study revealed positive relationship between use of consultancy and perceived enterprise performance. There is a significant and direct influence of use of consultancy on managerial competency of owner managers. Though attitudinal issues were perceived to be favourable to engage the consultants, the actual use of the same was found to be moderate. However, majority of them were using services of chartered accountants who were considered as their mentors.

Chitra Ramachandran[98] conducted a study on 202 leaders of self help group members of Madurai district in Tamil Nadu, with a view to understanding the impact of micro-enterprises on quality of life of the women which was measured in terms of their living standards. She observed that most of the women in micro enterprise wanted to reduce poverty and to share their family responsibilities. The survey demonstrated that quality of life of the rural women had substantially increased after the establishment of the Micro Enterprises successfully.

Jyotirmayee kar[99] conducted a study to asses credit needs of 212 small scale units selected from four major industrial estates namely Mancheswar, Jagatpur, Rourkela and Kalunge in the state of Orissa. It has been observed that most often it is the interplay of the business traits and ownership patterns which get as major determinants to the demand as well as the supply of credit. The empirical work also finds that the need for credit is observed to be increasing with investment requirement and the level of output ie., the scale of operation.

Panda[100] conducted an empirical research on the relationship that exists among various socio-economic variables with different success levels among the 212 small-scale units located in Orissa, Andhra Pradesh, Bihar and West Bengal. The findings revealed that there are associations between the success levels of an enterprise with factors like technical education of the entrepreneur, occupational background of parents, previous background of the entrepreneur and capability to arrange working capital. It also 00brings out the entrepreneurs perception of risk namely, the functional risk and business risk.

Bala Subrahmanya, Mathirajan and Balachandra[101] investigated the extent and magnitude of Research and Development(R&D) carried out by 2006 small firms in Karnataka. The results reveals that a significant number of small firms moved towards incremental innovations i.e., improving product quality by technical efforts, changing product designs to suit market needs and overcoming common problems as part of their R & D and innovations.

Rajendran[102] conducted a study on socio-economic backgrounds and influencing factors for successful entrepreneurial development in 89 entrepreneurs from south Andaman district. The results revealed that the majority of entrepreneurs do not have higher education, sole trading concerns and non-traditional business communities with own capital were forced to become entrepreneurs.

Panda[103] conducted a study to highlight the marketing practice followed by 78 small hotel entrepreneurs operating in the state of Nagaland, a developing state located in the north eastern part of India. It was found that sales activity in majority of the cases is managed by the hired managers follow market based pricing policy and charge a room rent at par with their competitions. It also revealed that the migrated entrepreneurs with higher education, previous occupation in politics, government service and business and a choice to offer full line service are the market leaders in the hotel industry of Nagaland.

Chawla, Batra and Amour[104] conducted a study focusing mainly examing the pattern of finance and its utilization by the 50 Small and Medium Enterprises(SMEs) operating in Rwanda. The financing of the SMEs is an economic necessity that has to be taken into consideration by the governments of Rwanda while formulating the policies. The pattern of investment in the SMEs in Rwanda is specially composed of a mix of equity and debt financing.

ENTREPRENEURSHIP AND ENTREPRENEURIAL STUDIES IN ANDHRA PRADESH

Two decades ago Gaikwad & Tripathy[105] studied in detail the enterprises of the well-known family of Mullapudi Harichandra Prasad in the West Godavari district. In addition they also examined the small entrepreneurs of the Tanuku region in the same District. For the main focus of their study, they selected ten other entrepreneurs who had started industries after 1947 and a purposive sample of 15 entrepreneurs in trade. The study revealed that all the entrepreneurs were persons with initiative; drive hard work, resolved on success though the majority of them had hardly any technical or economic base, or political connections. One interesting finding of their study is that even after realizing the scope for industrial development in the region, the traders of the area did not take to industrial entrepreneurship because, in their view, it required a large capital outlay, high managerial and organizational skills and technical knowledge. Moreover, they were not prepared to wait for returns as industries generally have a long gestation period.

The Small Industries Extension Training (SIET) Institute[106], Hyderabad conducted a survey of 61 small entrepreneurs situated in the twin cities of Hyderabad and Secunderabad, to investigate into the reasons which made them to start their units. The study revealed that "economic gains" was the most important reason for starting small industrial units and ambition, social prestige, and social responsibility came next in order. Apart from this, high demand for the product perceived, was the most encouraging factor. Capital shortages and Government red tapism were identified by the study as the most inimical factors. The study further revealed that younger age, formal education, urban background, experience in industry, high scores in levels aspirations, risk taking and adoption propensity were some of the negatively associated characteristics with entrepreneurship.

Nafziger[107] conducted a study of 54 entrepreneurs of small scale manufacturing enterprise in Visakhapatnam. He analyzed extensively the distribution of entrepreneurs by caste and class (parental, economic and occupational status) in relation to the total population of the city and related the performance of the entrepreneurs of the educational attainment, occupational background, managerial and entrepreneurial experiences, initial capital, access to governmental assistance and business success of the entrepreneurs. He used the value added of the firm and the income class of the entrepreneurs as the major indicators for business success. He arrived at two conclusions:

(i) Rich families succeeded as entrepreneurs due to education, work-experience access to capital and availability of government assistance.

(ii) The socio-economic status of businessmen was generally higher than that of the general population in the socialist countries.

Sarveswara Rao and Lakshamana Rao[108] conducted a study of commercial and industrial establishment in two areas of coastal A.P namely the Vijayawada, Guntur the Visakhapatnam-Anakapalli area. They focused attention on important socio-cultural variables like social community, regional origins, educational levels and family background as well as working of industrial and commercial enterprises. The study found that the average size of enterprise in the Industrial Estate was bigger than of the enterprises outside the Industrial Estate.

Sharma S.V.S[109] has detailed the research studies on entrepreneurial characteristics and their usefulness in identifying and selecting potential entrepreneurs, to formulate a strategy to develop entrepreneurship through interventions. The author opined that to arrive at a universally applicable and invariant portrait of an entrepreneur might not be possible. But, he held a view that in every society some possess entrepreneurial qualities to a greater degree than others and these people can be encouraged to take up entrepreneurial activity.

Gnana Kannan[110] advocated training not only for potential and existing entrepreneurs but also for persons who are directly or indirectly associated in promoting entrepreneurship like: (a) policy-makers, (b) Government executives, (c) Field personnel, (d) personnel of the support systems and (e) workers of Voluntary organizations. He prepared a course content of the training for both the groups.

Manohar Deshpande[111] has observed occupational mobility away from primary occupations in a study of entrepreneurship in Telengana region of AndraPradesh. Social factors like caste, family occupation and father's occupational status were found to be important to gain entry into industry.

Subbi Reddy and Sobha Reddy[112] discussed the entrepreneurial and economic dimensions of the profile of entrepreneurs in Kurnool district of Andhra Pradesh. They also presented at length the empirical studies conducted by many scholars in their paper. They concluded that the entrepreneur was a local young man with secondary education, he had previous experience in industry, business or government service. The entrepreneurs of Kurnool district have set up proprietary and partnership concerns. Nearly two thirds of them are Hindus and a majority of them belong to Vysya Community.

Chitra Rao and Mishra[113] attempted to make the selection procedure more systematic and scientific. A group planning exercise was added in order to test leadership abilities, learn spirit, commitment to task, planning and organizing ability and decision-making. They suggested multistage screening-method. They advocated designing simpler selection methods for such groups.

E. Desingu Setty[114] discussed the problems and prospects of promoting entrepreneurship in small industry. The problems were classified as individual, group and institutional. The author called for suitable support systems for each class of problems.

Fifty one entrepreneurs of the Krishna and Guntur districts were studied by Lakshmana Rao[115] with a view to finding out how far programmes and the policies of the government fostered industrial entrepreneurship. He was of the view that the government schemes did certainly give a boost to the growth of entrepreneurship in Andhra Pradesh.

The study of entrepreneurs operating in Indian Industrial Estates, with special reference to those in the Coastal regions of Andhra Pradesh, Gangadhara Rao[116] selected 87 entrepreneurs operating in 13 estates of coastal Andhra Pradesh. It was his observation that educational and income levels were important factors in motivating entrepreneurship. He found that, money making was the major ambition of the entrepreneurs. He came to the conclusion that the impact of Industrial Estate on the emergence of entrepreneurship in Coastal A.P was marginal.

Lakshmana Rao[117] in his work entitled "Industrial Entrepreneurship in India" highlighted the role of human factor in economic development and reviewed economic and non-economic theories of entrepreneurship. He presented results of his statistical analysis of data collected through a sample survey (Krishna and Guntur districts). He gave a detailed account of policies and programmes of the state and central government for promoting industrial entrepreneurship with focus on small scale sector.

In their study entitled "Entrepreneurship Development Programmes-an Evaluation" of the suitability of the candidates selected, Subbi Reddy and Appa Rao[118] discussed the impact of such a programme on selected candidates. They attempted to study the profile, problems, perceptions and aspirations of 30 candidates selected under Entrepreneurship Development Programme.

Narasimha Murthy[119] conducted a study to evaluate the growth enterprises in Anakapalle and Gudiwada, which are two small towns of Coastal Andhra Pradesh. On the basis of the entrepreneurial activities like farming, trading, manufacturing, profession etc., he sought to identify the socio-economic origins, to ascertain entrepreneurial process and promises, analyzed occupational and geographical mobility through generations and to high light their problems. Murthy holds the view that the Indian Society is witnessing a slow and gradual but sure transformation and the seeds of entrepreneurship are sprouting even in the hitherto less enterprising social segments. He found that the process of entrepreneurship has certainly accelerated.

K.Ravichandra[120] attempted a comparative study of the successful and unsuccessful entrepreneurs, in Hyderabad, in terms of social, educational and psychological characteristics, with a view to arriving at a profile of a potentially successful entrepreneur.

Pannalal[121] studied a sample of Industrial Estates in AndhraPradesh, and concluded: 1. Single proprietorship is not only popular but also successful followed by partnership, 2. Most of the entrepreneurs are in the age group 31-40 years, 3. Parent's background in industry, trade and contracts works is highly conducive for entrepreneurial career and 4. Engineering industries seem to thrive in the Industrial Estates, constituting as many as 62% of the sample.

Krishna Kumar[122] has analyzed that the economic development can be sustained through the process of industrialization, especially by developing the small industry by inculcating, the talents of entrepreneurship which result in augmenting the growth possibilities, so as to realize more values for investment while reducing the unemployment.

Jayachandran, G.,Vijayalakshmi.B.,and Hima Chalam, D.,[123] have indicated in their study that, the entrepreneurship development and that of the industrial development are two sides of the same coin. Therefore, the promotion of entrepreneurship can be done effectively through the development of small scale industries. They have stressed that, there is need to motivate, encourage and equip the entrepreneurs with the requisite technical, managerial and financial resources, so that they can become successful entrepreneurs and thereby promote the process of industrial development.

K. Madhumurthy[124] in his study of 80 entrepreneurs from Warangal, Visakhapatnam and Hyderabad found that 1. Agriculture and business families are the main sources of entrepreneurial supply, 2. Most of them are graduates, 3. Most of them are of age group between 26 to 30 years have started their entrepreneurship career, 4. Engineering graduates are having experience before starting, 5. The main motivational factors to choose entrepreneurial career are desire for independent life, personal fame, innovation and encouragement by government agencies.

Kalyani and Chandralekha[125] conducted a study on 300 women entrepreneurs in the Rayalaseema area (Anantapur, Chittoor, Cuddapah and Kurnool districts) of Andhra Pradesh, who take initiatives to start their own enterprises and also dwells upon the factors that motivate in launching of enterprise. The result reveals that various socio-economic and demographic characteristics have significant impact on involvement of women entrepreneurs in their enterprise management.

Kasi Reddy[126] conducted a study to know the various entrepreneurial activities among scheduled castes and scheduled tribes in 120 units selected from Ananthapur, Krishna and Ranga Reddy districts of Andhra Pradesh. The results revealed that most of the enterprises were established in the recent past, proprietary concerns and were producing industrial and intermediary goods and services.

SUMMARY

The review of literature indicated the growth and development of entrepreneurship and small scale enterprise is influenced by the socio-cultural factors and the support systems provided by the various governments. There is a common trend of the socio-cultural and economic factors which will play a catalytic role in furthering the development of entrepreneurship.

REFERENCES

1. Vepa, Ram.K.,Modern Small Industry in India, Sage Publications, New Delhi, 1988.
2. Atkins, M.H and Lowe, J. F., Sizing Up Small Firm : UK and Australian Experience, International Small Business Journal, 15(3), p. 42-55,1997.
3. Curran, James and Blackburn, R.A, Researching the Small Enterprise, Sage Publications : 1. London, 2001.
4. Resnik, P. The Small Business Bible: The Make or break factors survival and success, John Willey, New York, 1988.
5. Bolton, B and Thomson, J, "Entrepreneurs Talent Temperament, technique", Butterworth – Heinemann, Boston, 2000.
6. Haksever, C., Total Quality Management in the Small Business environment, Business Horizons 39 (2), 1996, p. 33-40.
7. Chachadi, A.H, Decision Making in Small Industry, Unpublished doctoral thesis, Karnataka University, Dharwad, 1988.
8. Penrose E T, The Theory of Growth of the Firm, Blackwell, Oxford, 1959.
9. Curran, James and Blackburn, R.A, op.cit.,
10. Burrows, R and Curran, J, Sociological research on service sector small business: some conceptual considerations work, Employment and Society, 3(4), 1989, p. 527–531.
11. Phansalkar, S J, How not to ruin your small industry, Sage Publications, New Delhi, 1996.
12. SBA Office of Advocacy, The Facts about Small Business, 1997, p.1.
13. Atkins, M H and Lowe, JF, op.cit.,
14. Haksever, C. op.cit.
15. Alexander.A.P., Greek Industrialists-An Economic and Social Analysis, Centre of Planning and Economic Research, Athens,1961.
16. Harris. John.R., "Nigerian Entrepreneurship," and "Nigerian Entrepreneurship in Industry", in Kilby(ed) Entrepreneurship and Economic Development, The Free Press, New York,1971.
17. Harris. John.R.," Nigerian Entrepreneurship in Industry", in Growth and Development in Nigerian Economy (ed) Eicher and lied Biokes, East Lausin Michigan University Press,1970, p.310.

18. Merris. Peter, The Social Barriers to African Entrepreneurship, Institute for Development Studies, University College, Nairobi, p.11.

19. Miracle.M., "Capitalism, Capital Markets and Competition in West Africa Trade" in Mellasoux .C., (ed) The Development of Indigenous Trade and Markets in West Africa, Oxford University Press, London, p. 402-403.

20. Schatz.Sayre., The Capital Shortage Illusion, Government spending In Nigerian, Oxford Unversity Press, 1965, p.3-10.

21. Kennedy.P., " Entrepreneurship in the Private and Public Sectors in China", Bulletin of Institute of Development Studies, Sussex, June, 1971, p.52-53.

22. Harris. John.R., op.cit.,

23. Kilby. Peter, Industrialization in a Open Economy, Nigeria, University Press, Cambridge.1969.

24. Yousif. A.Sayigh, Entrepreneurs of Lebanon: The Role of Business Leader in Developing Economy, Harvard University Press, Cambridge, 1962.

25. Yousif.A.Sayigh, "Cultural Problems and The Economic Development of the Arab World", in Bellah.R.N(ed), Religion and Progress in Modern Asia, The Free Press, New York, 1965.

26. Bert.F.Hoselitz, The Entrepreneurship Element in Economic Development, International Hand Book of Management, Mc Graw Hill, NewYork, 1965.

27. Higgins, Benjamin, Introduction to a Symposium on Entrepreneurship and Labour skills in Indonesian Economic Development, Yale University, South East Asia Studies, NewHavens,Conn.,1961.

28. Kroef.J.M.Van Der, "Entrepreneurs and Middle Class in Indonesia", Economic Development and Cultural Change, Vol.2, p.197-375.

29. John, J.Carroll, The Philippine Manufacturing Entrepreneur: Agent and Product of Change, Corroll University Press ITHACO, 1965.

30. Papanek Gustav.F., Pakistan's Development Social Goals and Private Incentives, Harvard University Press, Cambridge, Massachusetts, 1967.

31. Susumu Watanable, "Entrepreneurship and Small Enterprises in Japanese Manufacturing", International Labour Review, Vol.102, No.6, December 1970, p.570-571.

32. Sharma.S.V.S.Small Entrepreneurial Development in Some Asian Counties-A Comparative Study, Light and Life Publishers, New Delhi, 1979.

33. Bhattacharya. S.N., Entrepreneurship Development in India and the South-East Asian Countries, Light and Life Publishers, New Delhi, 1979.

34. Altaf.Zafar, Pakistani Entrepreneurs-Their Development Characteristics and Altitudes, IBD Publishers and Distributors, New Delhi, 1984.

35. Peter F. Drucker, Innovation and Entrepreneurship Practice and Principles, Heienemann, London, 1985.

36. Akhouri M.M.P, "Entrepreneurship and Small Industry Development-Experience form Asian Region" in the proceedings of the workshop Entrepreneurship and Small Enterprise Development: Policies and Strategies; Kingston, Jamaica, 26-30 March, 1990, p.271-343.

37. Umesh Patnaik.C, "Entrepreneurship Education in Canada: An observation," Sedme, Vol.21,June 1994, p.21-25.

38. Sukhpal Singh, " Refugees as Entrepreneurs: The case of the Indian Bicycle Industry," The Journal of Entrepreneurship, Vol.3, No.1, 1994, p. 85-86.

39. Cas Feng Qi, "Entrepreneurial Managers in China's Enterprise Reforms," China Business Issue, p.81-90, 1995.

40. Tyler, Sydney Scott, "Entrepreneurship and Small Business: A strategic management front and analysis", unpublished Ph.D., submitted to the Syracuse University, 1996.

41. Boliko, Mbuli, " New Perspectives in Entrepreneurship and SME Development": A Human Resource Management Approach (Small Scale Enterprise, Medium Scale Enterprises), unpublished Ph.D., submitted to the Nagoya University, Japan, 1996.

42. Li. Fang, "The Social Organization of Entrepreneurship: The rise of Private firms in China (Economic Reform)" unpublished Ph.D., submitted to the University of Chicago, Chicago, 1997.

43. Omoiele, M.Tambura, "African American Entrepreneurship: Socio-economic factors influencing success and failure", unpublished Ph.D submitted to the Union Institute, 1997.

44. Heidman, Marine Faith, "Moving to Entrepreneurship : An Exploration of Midlife Executive Women's Perceptions of their Transition into New Ways of Working (Job loss, informal working), unpublished Ph.D submitted to Michigan State University, 1997.

45. Steek, Charles N, "Entrepreneurship, Institutions and Economic Growth", New York University, New York, 1997.

46. Bellard, Anne-Marie, "The Role of Entrepreneurship in Reconstructing the Russian Economy", University of Nevade, Reno, 1997.

47. Selameab, Wolde Tsadik, "Factors impacting Entrepreneurial Behaviour among Graduates of Post-secondary Entrepreneurship programme(Small Businesses)", University of Minnesote, 1997.

48. Mitra,D.K., Bhatia, G.S., Pannuselvam, R., Maryth Powel, "Training Methodology and Inputs for Micro, Small and Medium Scale Enterprise in UK.", Sedme, Vol. XXIV, No. 2, June, 1997, p. 29-35.

49. Mark Casson, "Enterprise and Leadership" Edwar and Wlgar Publication, UK., 2000.

50. Richard. G.P. McMahon, 'Growth and Financial Profiles amongst Manufacturing SMEs from Australia's Business Longitudinal Survey', Entrepreneurship: Theory and Practice, Vol.26, No.2, 2001, p.51 - 61.

51. Honig, Benson, "Human Capital and Structural Upheaval: A Study of Manufacturing Firms in the West Bank", Journal of Business Venture, Vol.16, No.6, November, 2001, p.575-594.

52. Huang, Xueli, Soutar, Geoffrey, N. and Brown, Alan, 'New Product Development Processes in Small and Medium-sized Enterprises: Some Australian Evidence, Journal of Small Management, Vol 40, No.1, January, 2002, p.27-42.

53. Rolland Lebrasseur, Louis Zanibbi and Terrence J. Zinger, 'Growth Momentum in the Early Stages of Small Business start-ups', International Small Business Journal, Vol.21, No.3, August, 2003, p.315-330.

54. Bala Subrahmanya, M.H., 'Technological Innovations in Small Enterprises: Comparative Study of Bangalore and North-East England, Economic and Political Weekly, Vol.XXXVIII, No.21, May, 24-30, 2003, p.2067-2074.

55. Ayala Malach-pines, Dov Dvir, Arik Sadeh, "The Making of Israeli High-Technology Entrepreneurs: An Explanatory Study" The Journal

of Entrepreneurship, Sage Publications, New Delhi, January-June, 2004, p.29 - 52

56. Mitchell, B.C. "Motives of Entrepreneurs: A Case Study of South Africa", The Journal of Entrepreneurships, Sage Publications, New Delhi, July-December, 2004, p.167–183.

57. James T. McCrory, Case Studies in Latent Industries Potential: Small Industry in a North Indian Town, Ministry of Commerce and Industry, Government of India, Delhi, 1956.

58. Gadgil, D.R., The Industrial Evolution of India in Recent Times: 1860-1939, Oxford University Press, Bombay, 1971.

59. Gadgil, D.R., Origins of the Modern Indian Business Class-An Interim Report, International Secretariat, Institute of Pacific Relations, New York, 1959.

60. Andrew, F. Brimmer, The Settings of Entrepreneurship in India", The Quarterly Journal of Economics, November, 1955, p.553-576.

61. Berna, J.J., Industrial Entrepreneurship in Madras State, Asia Publishing House, Bombay, 1960.

62. UNESCO Research Centre, Social Aspects of Small Industries in India: Studies in Hawrah and Bombay, UNESCO Research Centre on Social and Economic Development in Southern Asia, Delhi, 1962.

63. Hanumantha Rao, K.S. and Sumithra, D.G., "Planning and the Growth of Industrial Entrepreneurship in India", The Indian Journal of Commerce, No.65, December, 1965, p.343-354.

64. Hazlehurst, L.W., Entrepreneurship and the Merchant Caste in a Punjab City ., Durham, D.C, Duke University, Common wealth Studies Center, 1966.

65. Amlendu Guha, "Parsi Seths and Entrepreneurs, 1750-1850", Economic and Political Weekly, Aug.29, 1970, p. M107-M115; and " The Comprador Role of Parsi Seths, 1750-1850", Economic and Political Weekly, November 28th, 1970, p.1933-1936.

66. Subramanian.R., Shiva Kumar.K., and Palanisami.M., Entrepreneurship in Small Industries in Madurai City and its Environs, Sangam Publishers, Madras, 1975.

67. Ashis Nandy and Raymond L. Owvens, The New Vysyas, Allied Publishers Pvt., Ltd, 1977.

68. Paul A.London, Merchants as Promoters of Rural Development, An Indian Case Study, Praeger Publishers, New York, 1978.

69. Moulik, T.K., Patel and Basu, Rural Entrepreneurship, Center for Management in Agriculture, Indian Institute of Management, Ahmadabad, 1978.

70. Sharma, R.A., Entrepreneurial Change in Indian Industry, Sterling Publications Pvt., Ltd., New Delhi, 1980.

71. Manohar U. Deshpande, Entrepreneurship of Small Scale Industries, Deep and Deep Publications, New Delhi, 1982.

72. Singh, P.N., Development Entrepreneurship for Economic Growth, Vikas Publishing House Pvt Ltd., New Delhi,1986.

73. Hadimani. R.N., Dynamics of Industrial Entrepreneurship, Ashish Publishing House, New Delhi, 1985.

74. Gupta, M.C., Entrepreneurship in Small Scale Industries, Anmol Publications, New Delhi, 1987.

75. Bhanushali.S.G., Entrepreneurship Development, An Interdisciplinary Approach, Himalaya Publication House, Bombay,1987.

76. Patel V.G, "Entrepreneurship Development Programs in India" in 'Development of New Entrepreneurs', EDII, Ahmedabad,1987, p.1-40.

77. Khanka.S.S, Entrepreneurship in Small Scale Industries, Himalaya Publishing House, Bombay, 1990.

78. Venkatachalam. R. and Saleendran, P.T, Innovation & Entrepreneurship Sedme, December,1990, p 53-57.

79. Tahera Mashauddin, "Personality Study of Successful and Unsuccessful Entrepreneurs", Sedme, June 1990, p. 143-155.

80. Narendra S. Bisht and Pamila K. Sharma, Entrepreneurship: Expectations and Experience, Himalaya Publication House, Bombay, 1991.

81. Louks, Kenneth, Training Entrepreneurship for Small Business Creation: Lessons from experience. ILO Geveva, Oxford and IBH Publishing Co.Pvt.Ltd,1991, p.12.

82. Ashis Gupta, "Indian Entrepreneurial Culture: Bengal and Eastern India" in 'The Culture of Entrepreneurship' Ed.by Brigitte Berger, The Tata McGraw-Hill publishing Company Ltd., New Delhi, 1992, p.99-136.

83. Kanitkar A, "Integrating the Extension Approach in Entrepreneurship developing activities: Rationale, Experience and Issues", Sedme, Vol.21, No.2, June ,1992,p.1-19.

84. Chandra R.K, Entrepreneurial Success: A Psychological Study, New Delhi: Sterling Publishers, 1991.

85. Vinayshil Gautham., "Towards Developing a Science and Technology based Entrepreneurship Index" in 'Technical Entrepreneurship : Issues of Research & Application' Ed. Vinayshil Gautham,Global Business Press, New.Delhi, 1992, p.48-55.

86. Ravi.K.Zutshi., "Role of Technical Entrepreneurs in Industrial Development- An alternative View" in Technical Entrepreneurship: Issues of Research &Application(Ed) Vinayshil Gautham, Global Business Press, New Delhi, 1992, p.13-24.

87. Sarangadharam.M and Razia Begum, "Women Entrepreneurship : Institutional support and Problems, Discovery Publishing House, New Delhi, 1995, p. 15.

88. Jawahar.R.M.P, "Entrepreneurship Development in a Science Park", Sedme, Vol.20, No.3, September, 1994, p.15-21.

89. Kamala Singh, "Women Entrepreneurs", Ashish Publishing House, New Delhi, 1992, p.169-175.

90. Ahluwalia.I.J " Industrial Policy and Industrial Performance in India", Lucas & D.Robert and Papanek F.Gustav,Ed.The Indian Economy, Delhi: Oxford University Press, 1998.

91. Prabath, S.V., Entrepreneurship Development in India a Review, Sedme, Vol. XXIV, No. 3, September, 1997, p.1-5.

92. Lillian Vernonkatz, the characteristics of a successful Entrepreneur, Journal of Economic Literature, Vol.38, No.1, 1998, p. 64-72.

93. Chandrapoojary, Entrepreneurship Pull & Push Effect, Sedme Vol. XXIV, September, 1999, p.11-18.

94. Ranjeeth, Asthana, K. Entrepreneurship Development Yojana, Vol. 42, No.8, August, 1998, p. 61-62.

95. Sallappan R, Venkatapathy, R, Entrepreneurial Awareness and Practice among students , Sedme, Vol. XXV, No.2, June, 1998, p. 47-57.

96. Anitha, H.S., Laxmishra, A.S., Women Entrepreneurship in India, Southern Economist, Vol. 38, No. 4, June, 1999, p.11-13.

97. Vasudev Rao A.S., "Growth and Development of Small Enterprise Consultancy – Problems and Prospects" unpublished Ph.D., submitted to Karnataka University, Dharwad, 2003.

98. Chitra Ramachandran, " Status of Women Entrepreneurs who established micro entrepreneurs in Madurai District" Unpublished Ph,D., Madurai Kamaraj University, Madurai, 2005.

99. Jyotirmayee kar, "Credit, Demand and Supply: A Study of Small-Scale Units" The Journal of Entrepreneurship, Sage Publications, New Delhi, July, December, 2002, p.191 – 218

100. Tapan K. Panda, "Entrepreneurial success and Risk perception among Small-Scale Entrepreneurs of Eastern India, The Journal of Entrepreneurship, Sage Publications, New Delhi, July-December, 2002, p.173 - 190.

101. Bala Subrahmanya, M.H, Mathirajan, M and Balachandra.P, 'R & D Behaviour Objectives and Performance of Small Scale Industries in Karnataka' Sedme, Vol.29, No.1, March, 2002, p. 1 - 17.

102. Rajendran, G, ' A Study on the Entrepreneurial Development in Andaman and Nicobar Islands', Sedme, Vol.29, No.4, December, 2002, p.61 - 65

103. Panda, N.M, 'Marketing Management in Small Service Enterprises: A case study of Hotel Industry in Nagaland', Sedme, Vol.30, No.2, June 2003, p.55 - 70

104. Chawla, A.S., Batra, G.S., and Dufatanye Jean d'Amour, 'Financing Practices and Problems of Small and Medium Enterprises in Rwande', Sedme, Vol.31, No.4, December, 2004, p.1 - 18

105. Gaikwad.V.R., and Tripathy.R.N., Socio-Psychological Factors Influencing Industries Entrepreneurship in Rural Areas, National Institute of Community Development, Hyderabad,1970.

106. SIET, Socio-Psychological Factors Influencing and Adoption of the Innovation of starting a Small Industry Unit, SIET Institute, Hyderabad, 1974.

107. Nafziger.F.W., Class, Caste and Entrepreneurship- A Study of Indian Industrialists, An East West Centre, The University Press of Hawali, Honululu, 1978.

108. Sarveswara Rao.B., and Lakshamana Rao.V., " Industrial and Commercial Entrepreneurship in the Coastal Region of A.P", ICSSR Research Abstracts Quarterly, Oct-Dec.,1978, p.31-58.

109. Sharma.S.V.S. "Characteristics of Entrepreneurs" in 'Development of Entrepreneurship Issues and Problems', SIET, Hyderabad, 1980, p.71-85.

110. Gnana.Kannan, "Training for Entrepreneurship Development" in 'Development of Entrepreneurship Issues and Problems', SIET, Hyderabad, 1980, p.117-130.

111. Manohar.U Deshpande, "Entrepreneurship of Small Industries-Concept, Growth and Management", Deep&Deep publications, New Delhi, 1982.

112. Subbi Reddy, T and Sobha Reddy.N., Profile of Small Entrepreneurs in Kurnool, Sedme, Vol. XI, March, 1994, p.39-49.

113. Chitra Rao and Mishra S.P, " Selection of Potential Entrepreneurs – An Appraisal of Methodologies ", Sedme, September, 1985, p. 25 – 31.

114. E.Desingu Setty, " Promoting Small Entrepreneurship: Problems and Prospects" in 'Developing Entrepreneurship: Issues and Problems',SIET, Hyderabad, 1980, p.23-34.

115. Lakshamana Rao.V, Industrial Entrepreneurship in India, Chugh Publications, New Delhi, 1986.

116. Gangadhara Rao.N., Entrepreneurship and Growth of Enterprise in Industrial Estates, Deep & Deep Publications, New Delhi, 1986.

117. Lakshmane Rao. V, Industrial Entrepreneurship in India, Chugh Publications, Allahabad, 1986.

118. Subbi Reddy. T and Appa Rao. P. B, Entrepreneurship Development Programme – An Evaluation of the suitability of the candidates selected, (memeo), Pandu vennela prachuranahi, Anantapur, 1987.

119. Narasimha Murthy.B.E.V.V., Entrepreneurship in Small Towns, Mittal Publications, New Delhi,1989.

120. Ravi Chandra.K, "Entrepreneurial Success: A Psychological Study" Sterling Publishers Pvt, Ltd., New Delhi, 1991.

121. Pannalal, "Status of Small Scale Enterprises in Industrial Estates in Andhra Pradesh: A Study", Sedme, Vol.21, No.4, December, 1994, New Delhi, p.57-58.

122. Krishna Kumar, Entrepreneurial Success: An Empirical Study in Mahaboob Nagar District, Sedme, Vol. XXV, 1997, p. 30-34.

123. Jayachandran, G, Vijayalakhsmi,B., Hima Chalam.D., Entrepreneurial Profile in Industrial Estate A study, Sedme, Vol. XXIV, No.2, September, 1997, p. 9-14.

124. Madhu Murthy.K, "Some Aspects of Entrepreneurship Development in Developing Economics with specific reference to India", Unpublished Ph.D, Kakatiya University, Warangal, 1997.

125. Kalyani, W., Chandralekha, K., "Association between socio-economic Demographic Profile and Involvement of Women Entrepreneurs in their Enterprise Management", the Journal of Entrepreneurship, Sage Publications, New Delhi, July – December, 2002, p. 219–248.

126. Kasi Reddy, M, 'Profile of Scheduled Caste and Scheduled Tribe Entrepreneurs in Andhra Pradesh: An Empirical Study' Sedme, Vol.30, No. 2, June 2003, p. 71-78.

3

RESEARCH METHODOLOGY

INTRODUCTION

Research on small scale entrepreneurship is distinctive, hence decision on selection of methodology and design for small scale entrepreneurship research poses specific challenges. This chapter has elaborated the research methodology and research design used in the study. From the point of view of the purpose, this study is primarily descriptive in nature. The researcher has tried to present a scientific description of a variety of facts pertaining to small scale entrepreneurship, their socio-economic factors, the nature of motivational factors, the growth factors, opinions about globalization and liberalization the nature of problems faced and opinion on variety of aspects to their entrepreneurial success including the future plans.

The research design includes developing sample frame, practical procedures for examining the respondents of the research, and the methods used for data collection and analysis. This chapter describes the methodology with the following sections.

1. Basic Research Questions.
2. Sampling Frame and Samples.
3. Survey Instrument Used.

4. Data Collection
5. Data Analysis Methods.

BASIC RESEARCH QUESTIONS

Based on the literature review discussed in Chapter 2 a set of research questions framed for the current study are as follows.

1. What are the motivational factors behind entrepreneur to go for entrepreneurship?
2. What are the opinions of entrepreneur regarding globalization and liberalization?
3. What are the problems faced by the small scale entrepreneurs?

As mentioned earlier, a descriptive research design is being used for the study. However, as a part of the study, cross relationships between variables have been examined at several places. Hypotheses regarding the existence of relationships between the variables were constructed in each case and were tested. However, these hypotheses are not being listed under a separate heading of "Hypotheses", for the simple reason that such a separate listing might give an impression that these are the central concerns of the study. In fact, dwelving into the search for some relationships was also a part of this broadly descriptive exercise and, therefore, in order to retain the focus, only the objectives and the basic research questions have been mentioned here.

SAMPLING FRAME AND SAMPLES

A field survey was conducted for data collection from a sample size of 196 small scale entrepreneurs located in Nellore district, a coastal district in Andhra Pradesh.

Sampling Frame: As on 31-3-2004, Nellore district had a total number of 20978 small scale enterprises according to the data furnished by the District Industries Centre, Nellore district. Large number of them were tiny industries and small service-based enterprises, having much lower capital investment of Rs. 1,00,000 and less. These were mainly self–employment oriented enterprises having entrepreneurs working themselves or along with less than about five employees. Such units did not essentially constitute the target population for the study, as their life span was very limited. Such units were catering to the market needs and customers mostly belonging to the locality or the villages or nearby towns.

In order to meet the objectives, the present study designed a sample frame work based on the following broad criteria.

1. The small scale enterprises located in four Industrial Estates in Nellore (Andhra Pradesh Industrial Estate, Wood Complex, Auto nagar phase I, Auto nagar phase II), Industrial Estate, Gudur; Industrial Estate, Kavali; Industrial Developing Area, Pannemgedu; Integrated Industries Development Centre, Tada and Industrial Developing Area, Venkatachalam developed by state development agencies such as Andhra Pradesh Industrial Infrastructural Corporation (APIIC) and District Industries Centre (DIC) are considered for target population.
2. The units having capital investment (initial) of Rs. 1, 00,000 and above are considered.
3. The manufacturing units are only selected for the study.
4. The units which were started before 2001 and working currently are considered.
5. Sick and closed units are excluded, because of difficulty in obtaining relevant data.

Considering the criteria indicated above, a sample frame was designed, based on the data collected from District Industries Centre and Andhra Pradesh Industrial Infrastructural Corporation directories. A total of 653 units were short listed as target population for the study. Suggestions were sought from Small Industries Association, Nellore and District Industries Centres in Nellore to decide the sampling frame.

Sample Size: Out of 653 Units in the final sample frame, a 30 percent of the population was considered to determine the sample size. The sample units were selected randomly resulting in a sample size of 196 units.

The selected respondents mostly belonged to the manufacturing industries like automobile spare parts, metallurgical industries, chemicals, pharmaceuticals, engineering and electrical etc., It is important to recognize that these categories of manufacturing industries are the predominant type of small scale enterprises in the district.

Design: The research design choice, particularly for small scale enterprises, depends on the kind of problems being studied. Here descriptive research design may suit research topics for small enterprises.

Method: The method used for the study is field survey and interviews. Mailing of questionnaires, based on the earlier experiences of the researcher, could not yield adequate response. There were practical difficulties for the same, as the owner–managers are very reluctant or unwilling to share the data over telephone. Initial contact was established to ascertain prima facie willingness of the respondents to participate in the field survey. In case of the selected units not responding to the survey, replacement units had to be selected. However care was taken to avoid sampling bias as far as possible.

SURVEY INSTRUMENT USED

The survey instrument (i.e., questionnaire) was developed by focusing on general information of the enterprise, socio–economic factors, motivational factors, growth factors and problems encountered. The questionnaire was divided into six major parts.

The Part–I consisted of 10 questions to elicit the socio–economic variables of entrepreneur and his enterprise, enterprise start up, form of organization, sex, age, caste, marital status, education qualification of respondent and his father's annual income. The questions are developed with multiple choices.

In part II, 6 questions were framed focusing on motivational factors behind the entrepreneur. The questions were developed with multiple choices and some had statements with dichotomy answers.

Part III measured the growth factors in relation to investment, human resources, profitability and marketing. The questions had multiple choices.

In part IV had 3 questions focused on impact of globalization and liberalization on small scale entrepreneurship. The questions were developed on five point Likert scale and some had statements with dichotomy answers.

Part V had 9 questions on major problems encountered by small scale entrepreneurs. The questions were developed on five point Likert scale and some with dichotomy answers.

Part VI had 7 questions on opinions of entrepreneurial success by the entrepreneur. The questions were developed on five point Likert scale, multiple choices and with dichotomy answers.

A pilot study and focused group interview was conducted to test comprehensiveness and validity of the instrument. The focused group discussion were held with small scale enterprise owner–managers, small enterprise association office bearers, general managers of District Industries Centers and Andhra Pradesh Industrial Infrastructural Corporation, and also managers of Commercial banks. The final questionnaire was designed based on the feed back from the pilot study

DATA COLLECTION

The instrument used in the study was intended to solicit the responses from the owner managers of respondent units and generally arrive at a pattern of solutions to the problems, or answers to the questions. By self administering the questionnaire, the researcher collected the data from the respondents. The follow up was done through frequent visits and face–to–face interviews.

The researcher personally visited the sample units located mainly in the Industrial Estates in Nellore(APIE, Wood Complex,

Autonagar phase I and Autonagar phase II),Gudur, Kavali, Pannemgedu, Tada and Venkatachalam.

Secondary data were collected from the offices of the District Industries Centre, Nellore, National Institute of Small Industry Extension Training (NISIET), Hyderabad and Andhra Pradesh Industrial Infrastructural Corporation (APIIC), Nellore. Besides, various publications of Government of India such as Census of Small Scale Industries, Economic Survey, Report on Small Enterprises (Abid Hussain Committee), Bulletins of Reserve Bank of India, were used to collect relevant secondary data pertaining to macro–scenario of small scale enterprises, definitions, performance, category of small enterprises' problems etc.,

For literature, the researcher had gone through various books, journals, websites, research reports, magazines and newspapers on small scale industry and entrepreneurship available in the libraries of the Department of Management Studies, Sri Venkateswara University, Tirupathi, Indian Institute of Management, Bangalore, Sri Krishnadevaraya University, Ananthapur, University of Madras, Chennai and Osmania University, Hyderabad.

DATA ANALYSIS METHODS

Data collected through a structured questionnaire were analyzed to find out the socio economic factors, motivational factors, growth factors and impact of globalization and liberalization as well as problems encountered in small scale enterprises. Since the researcher visited the respondent units personally for data collection, all the 196 units responded to the questionnaires. The response from these 196 respondents constitutes the primary data for the current study. The data are presented in the form of simple and bivariate Tables.

The statistical tools were used, as and when necessary, for the analysis of the data. These include percentages, mean, median, mode, standard deviations, Chi-square, Z-test and variances were examined with the use of ANOVA test.

SCOPE AND LIMITATIONS OF THE STUDY

The limitations of this study are as follows.

1. The study has included the industries in industrial estates only, certain traditional industries located outside the industrial estate such as fisheries, aquaculture, beedi manufacture (a tobacco based industry), small cashew processing units, tile manufacturing units, ice and cold storage plants etc., were excluded.
2. Most of the entrepreneurs were not interested to disclose the financial data.

SUMMARY

In a nutshell, the research methodology used was a sample survey method. The sample size consisted of 196 small scale enterprises located mainly in industrial estates of Nellore district. Structured questionnaire was self administered for data collection and follow up was done through personal visits and interview.

The responses collected were analyzed using statistical techniques such as frequency distribution, cross tabulation chi square and ANOVA.

4

SOCIO–ECONOMIC PROFILE OF THE STUDY REGION

INTRODUCTION

This chapter presents the socio- economic profile of India, the state of Andhra Pradesh and the Nellore district which is chosen for the study.

THE STATE OF INDIAN ECONOMY

The objective of this section is to provide background for understanding entrepreneur operating in Indian economy during the post–Independence period. India is the seventh largest and the second most populous nation of the world. India's population was 1027 million as on March 1, 2001, constitutes nearly 16.89 per cent of the total world's estimated population of 6080 million in 2000 [1] while her geographical area (about 3.29 million sq. km) is only 2.42 per cent of the world area (135.79 million sq. km). India lies entirely in the northern hemisphere as the mainland of India extends between latitudes 8° 4' N and 37° 6'N. On its northern frontiers, India is bounded by the great Himalayas. It stretches south wards and beyond the tropic of cancer, it narrows down to form the Great Indian Peninsula which ends up in the Indian ocean with cape comorin (Kanyakumari) as its southern most tip. On the east of the peninsular India is the Bay of Bengal, where in lie the Indian islands of Andaman and Nicobar, and on the west is the Arabian sea with another, group of Indian islands called the Lakshadweep. India has a land frontier of 15,200 kilometers and a coastline of 7,516.6 kilometers including the mainland's coastline as well as that of the Indian islands[2].

The country has a long history spanning over five thousand years of human habitation, and a rich cultural heritage handed down by the native pre–Aryan, the Aryan and the invading civilizations. Her civilization is one of the most ancient with a glorious heritage. Today, she is the largest democracy of the world with a republican constitution. The climate contrasts, the varied land scapes and the widely divergent environmental conditions of India account for the magnificence of its flora and fauna. The vast variety of natural resources, ranging from rich soils and rare earth deposits, have provided a base for diversified economic activities which include over two thousand years old traditional agriculture and the new saga of modern industrialization generating numerous social-economic and cultural diversities.

India embarked upon planned economic development soon after the achievement of Independence. On the eve of the First Plan (1951-56), the industrial development in India was confined largely to the consumer goods sector (cotton textiles, sugar, salt , soap, leather goods and paper). Industries manufacturing , intermediate product's like coal, cement, steel, power, alcohol, non-ferrous metals, chemicals etc. were also established but their production was small as productive capacity was considerably below the requirements (except cement). Accordingly, only Rs.55 crores, out of the total expenditure of Rs.1,960 crores (a mere 2.8 percent) was spent on 'industry and minerals'. A number of industries were either set up in the public sector or started production which include Hindustan shipyard, Hindustan Machine Tools, Hindustan Antibiotics, Integral Coach Factory, Uttar Pradesh Government Cement Factory etc.,[3]

The Second Plan (1956-61) accorded top priority to programmes of industrialization as would be clear from the fact that the expenditure on industry and minerals was hiked to Rs. 938 crores under this plan which was 20.1 percent of the total expenditure of Rs.4,672 crores. Based on Mahelanobis Model, the Second Plan set out the task of establishing basic and capital goods industries on a large scale so that a strong base for industrial development in the future could be built. Three steel plants of one million tonnes ingot capacity each were set up in the public sector at Bhilai, Rourkela and Durgapur, besides the expansion and modernization programmes undertaken in the private sector. Third Five Year Plan (1961-66) also pressed forward with the establishment of basic capital and producer goods industries – with special emphasis on machine building programme-so that the growth of the economy in the subsequent plans could become self sustaining. As a result, expansion and diversification of capacity of the heavy engineering and machine building industries, castings and forgings , alloys tool and special steels, iron and steel and ferro–alloys and steps to increase the output of fertilizers and petroleum products were undertaken. Expenditure on industry was Rs.1, 726 crores which was 20.1 percent of the total expenditure of Rs. 8,577 crores under this Plan.

The Fourth Plan (1969-74) intended to complete industrial projects undertaken in the Third Plan. It also aimed to enlarge capacities in export promotion and import substitution industries. Out of the total expenditure of Rs.15,779 crores, industry received Rs.2,864 crores (18.2 percent of the total) in this plan. Programmes of industrial development in the Fifth Plan (1974-78) were formulated keeping in view the objectives of self-reliance and growth with social justice. 124 items were exclusively reserved for small scale industries and initiated an intensive programme for the development of ancillary industries as feeder industries to large scale units. The expenditure on industry was hiked to 22.8 percent (Rs.8,989 crores out of total of Rs. 39,426 crores) in the plan.

In a review of industrial development over the thirty years of planning, the Sixth Plan (1980-85) noted that industrial production had increased by about 5 times during this period . This plan emphasized optimum utilization of existing capacities and improvement of productivity, enhancement of manufacturing capacity, special attention to the capital goods industry and electronics industry improvement in energy efficiency , dispersal of industry etc., Of the total expenditure of Rs.1,09,292 crores under this Plan, the share of the industrial sectors was Rs.15,002 crores which comes to 13.7 percent. The period of the Sixth Plan brought wide range of changes in the industrial policy of the government. The industrial and trade policies were substantially liberalized.

The overall outlay envisaged in the Seventh Plan (1985-90) for industrial and mineral progammes in the public sector was Rs.19,663 crores. As against this, the actual expenditure was Rs.25,971 crores which in 11.9 percent of the total expenditure of Rs.2,18,730 crores in this Plan. As far as the Eighth Plan (1992-97) is concerned, the overall outlay for industrial and mineral programmes in the public sector was kept at Rs.40,588 crores. This was only 9.3 percent of the total outlay of Rs. 4,34,100 crores in the plan. This reduced allocation to industry and minerals in the Eight Plan is in line with liberalization measures announced in the New Industrial Policy of 1991, according to which, the private sector was destined to play an increasingly important role in industrial activities, especially in those fields where security and strategic or social considerations are not important. The public sector is expected to concentrate increasingly on basic and core sectors. The actual expenditure on industry during the Eight Plan period was just Rs.40,623 crores out of the total plan expenditure Rs.4,85,457 crores. This comes to just 8.4 percent of the total expenditure under this Plan[+]. It sought to achieve the desired growth in different sectors primarily through modifications in industrial trade, fiscal policies and changes in duties and taxes rather than through quantitative restriction on imports/exports or licensing mechanism. The plan envisaged a growth of 7.3 percent per annum in the manufacturing sector. This target was achieved as the actual rate of growth turned out to be 7.4 percent per annum.

The Ninth Plan (1997-2002) outlay for industry and minerals was kept at Rs. 65,148 crores. This was 7.6 percent for the total Plan outlay of Rs. 8,59,200 crores. However, the actual expenditure on industry and minerals in this Plan is expected to be only Rs.44,695 crores which is just 4.7 percent of total actual expenditure of Rs.9,41,041 crores in the plan[5]. The actual growth rate in the Ninth Plan was only 5.0 percent per annum, much less than the targeted growth rate of 8.2 percent per annum.

Table 1
Average Annual Growth Rate of Industrial Production (Use Based) in Pre-reform and Post –reform Decade

Used based or Functional Classification	*1980-81 to 1991-92**	*Eighth plan* 1992-93 to 1996-97*	*Ninth Plan* 1997-98 to 2001-02*	*2000-01*	*2001-02*
(1)	*(2)*	*(3)*	*(3)*	*(4)*	*(5)*
Basic Goods	7.4	6.8	4.1	3.7	2.6
Capital Goods	9.4	8.9	4.7	1.8	-3.4
Intermediate Goods	4.9	8.5	5.8	4.7	1.5
Consumer Goods	6.0	6.6	5.5	8.0	6.0
Durables	10.8	13.4	10.7	14.5	11.5
Non-durables	5.3	4.8	3.8	5.8	4.1
General Index	**7.8**	**7.4**	**5.0**	**5.0**	**2.7**

*Simple average of the annual growth rates.

Sources : (i). For Column (2), Government of India , Economic Survey, 2000-01, Box 7.1 , p.130. (ii). For Column (3), Reserve Bank of India, Hand book of Statistics on Indian Economy, 2000, Table 199, p.409 and (iii). For other Columns, Government of India, Economic survey , 2002-03, Table 7.3, p.131.

The Tenth Five Year Plan (2002-07) proposed an outlay of Rs.58,939 crores for industry and minerals which in just 3.9 percent of the total outlay of Rs.15,25,639 crores[6]. The reduced allocation to industry is in line with the government's strategy to liberalize and privatize and give more space to the private sector to expand its activities. The plan sets an ambitious target of 10 percent per annum growth for the industrial sector. The onus of realizing this target lies on the private sector as the role of the public sector is slated to decline considerably.[7]

The year 1991 ushered in a new era of economic liberalisation. Major liberalisation measures designed to affect the performance of the industrial sector. The Table 1 which compares the performance of the industrial sector during the pre-reform decade and post–reform decade follows.

As it is clear from this Table 1, the rate of growth of industrial production was lower in the post–reform decade as compared with the pre-reform decade. A comparison of data in columns (3) and (4) shows that the performance during the latter half of 1990s (the Ninth Plan Period) deteriorated considerably as compared with the first half of 1990s (the Eighth Plan Period). The rate of growth of industrial production in the Eighth Plan was 7.4 percent per annum which was the same as the targeted rate of growth. Thus the performance was satisfactory on this account. But in the Ninth Plan was only 5.0 percent against 8.2 percent per annum which was highly unsatisfactory. The industrial sector registered a dismal performance in the last year of the Ninth Plan, 2001-02 , with its rate of growth being just 2.7 percent. This is the worst performance over the entire decade 1992-93 to 2001-02 excepting the year 1992-93 when the rate of industrial growth was 2.3 percent.

As far as sector wise growth is concerned, a glance at Table 1 shows that the performance of capital goods sector and basic goods sector has deteriorated in 1990s as compared with 1980s. The intermediate goods sectors and the consumers' goods sectors put up a better performance in the post–reform decade as compared with the pre-reform decade. Consumer durables are the only sector to have witnessed double–digit growth both in the pre-reform decade and the post–reform decade. The above analysis clearly shows that the performance of the industrial sector during the post–reform period has been highly unsatisfactory. In this context, Chaudhuri has calculated the compound annual rate of growth (CARG) of gross value added by the registered manufacturing sector over the period 1950-51 to 1998-99. His study shows that the rate of growth of gross value added in industry during 1990-91 to 1998-99 was just 5.91 percent per annum i.e., lower than the rate of growth of 7.47 percent annum registered during the Second and Third Five Year Plans (when a conscious effect was made to develop the basic and heavy industries) and the rate of growth of 7.66 percent per annum registered during the period of 1980s (when an attempt was made to reform the control mechanism without totally negating the role of the government)[8]. This is despite the fact that there was an investment boom in the first half of 1990s(as is evidenced from the fact that the average of the annual growth rate of gross fixed capital formation which was about 10 percent per year in the 1980s rose to over 15 percent per year between 1991-92 and 1996-97)[9].

Nagaraj's study shows that there is no evidence of a statistically significant improvement in the registered manufacturing growth rates in any of the 17 major states of India after the reforms. In fact, the growth rates in registered manufacturing in four states Bihar, Punjab, Haryana and Uttar Pradesh witnessed statistically significant slowdown after the reform (for instance, the growth rate in registered manufacturing fell from 11.7 percent during 1981-91 to 3.7 percent during the entire period 1981-98 in the case of Bihar; from 9.7 percent to 8.7 percent over the same period in the case of Punjab; from 8.6 percent to 6.9 percent in the case of Haryana; and from 14.2 percent to 8.5 percent in the case of Uttar Pradesh)[10].

Steps for development of small–scale and cottage industries were initiated immediately after Independence. For this purpose, a Cottage Industries Board was set up in 1947 itself. This was split into three boards during the First Five Year Plan–All India Handloom Board, All India Handicrafts Board and All India Khadi and Village Industries Board. In addition, three more boards were set up. These were the Small Scale Industries Board, Coir Board and Central Siik Board. Actual expenditure on small scale industries in the First Plan was Rs.42 crores. This rose to Rs.187 crores in the Second Plan. The programme of Industrial estates was initiated in 1955. It was extended in the second plan and about 60 industrial estates were set up for providing factory accommodation and a number of common facilities like power, water, transport etc., at one place. The actual expenditure during the Third Plan was estimated at Rs.241 crores and during the Annual Plans (1966-69) at Rs.132 crores. The Government failed to protect the small industries from the competition of large – scale industries in this plan. The Fourth Plan while admitting this fact cautioned the government..Besides, the reservation of items to be produced exclusively by the small scale sector, the major commercial banks of the country were nationalized to cater to the credit needs of the small scale sector. The estimated out lay in the public sector for village and small industries worked out to be Rs.251 crores in the Fourth Plan. Besides, the total amount of investment in the private sector exceeded the target of Rs.560 crores envisaged in the Fourth Plan[11].

Fifth Plan was to facilitate to remove poverty and inequality in consumption standards of the persons who depend on traditional industries. The estimated expenditure on village and small industries aggregated to Rs.388 crores. The Industrial Policy Statement of 1977 introduced the concept of District Industries Centres (DICs) for the promotion of small scale industries, to provide under a single roof all services and support required by the entrepreneurs and artisans. The government also initiated the 'nucleus industry' programme, the idea being that there should be an emphasis on the development of a core unit around which a nucleus of small units can grow in each area, hitherto deprived of Industrial activity. The core units were to offload at least 50 percent of the total manufacturing programme to ancillaries, to be developed with in the area and the concept of 'tiny sector', the smallest of the small sector, was introduced.

The Sixth Plan allocated a sum of Rs.1,952 crores for village and small industries. In 1982, Council for Advancement of Rural Technology (CART) was set up to provide the necessary technical input to the rural industries. The outlay for the small scale and cottage was kept at Rs.2,752.7 crores in the Seventh Plan whereas actual expenditure amounted to Rs.3,249 crores . The government announced its policy towards the small sectors on 6th August 1991. The main features of the Policy were: The small scale industrial sector has emerged as a dynamic and vibrant sector of the economy, during the eighties. At the end of Seventh Plan Period, it accounted for nearly 35 percent of the gross value of output in the manufacturing sector and over 40 percent of the total exports from the country. It also provided employment opportunities to around 12 million people.

The primary objective of the small sector industrial policy during the nineties was to impart more vitality and growth–impetus to the sector to enable it to contribute its mite fully to the economy, particularly in terms of growth of output, employment and exports. The outlay for village and small–scale industries in the Eight Plan was kept at Rs 6,334 crores. The actual expenditure on these industries during the plan amounted to Rs.7,266 crores.

Under the Scheme of Integrated Infrastructure Development Centres (IIDCs) launched in March 1994, infrastructure facilities are being developed in backward rural areas. 50 such IIDCs were to be set up during the Eight Plan Period, out of which 22 have been approved. This scheme was continued during the Ninth Plan with more incentives and financial assistance, including making available credit to facilitate its growth and development leading to increased contribution to output, exports and employment generation[12]. To provide technological support and training to small scale sector, tool rooms with German, Danish and Italian assistance are being set up at Indore, Ahmebabed, Bhubneshwar, Jamshedpur and Aurangabad.

Although growth has strong poverty reducing effects, the frictions and rigidities in the Indian economy can make these processes less effective, and the Tenth Plan was therefore formulated in a manner which-explicitly addresses the need to ensure equity and social justice. The government intends to spend Rs.7.754 crores on the village and the small industries (VSI) sector during the Tenth Plan. This includes Rs. 2,085 crores allocated for Khadi & Village industries. Overall performance of small–scale industries (SSI) over the period 1994-95 to 2001-03 has been provided in the Table 2[13].

The data reveal that the total number of SSI units has increased from 79.6 lakhs in 1994-95 to 110.1 lakhs in 2002-03 indicating an annual average growth rate of 4.1 percent, but their production (at 1993-94 prices) increased from Rs. 1,09,116 crores in 1994-95 to Rs. 2,10,636 crores in 2002-03 i.e., an annual average growth of 8.6 percent. As a consequence of the increase in SSI units, especially more in the unregistered sector, employment increased from 191.4 lakhs in 1994-95 to 266.4 lakhs in 2002-03, recording an average growth rate of 4 percent annum. So, as far as exports by the SSI sector are concerned, they were increased from Rs.29,068 crores in 1994-95 to Rs. 86,013 crores in 2002-03, recording a growth rate of 14.5 percent per annum and of employment by 4.0 percent.

Underutilization of human resources including entrepreneurial skills is the surest diagnosis of the ailing Indian Economy. There have been very rare instances where a development process has been initiated just by an accident. In this regard, it has to be stressed that the quality and quantity of human resources, which include among other, entrepreneurial ability, skilled manpower, the state of administration and national character are the prerequisites in order to change the initial conditions of the economy, however, entrepreneurship may not be regarded as a sufficient condition for growth activity, but it is surely a necessary condition.

The Ministry of Small Scale Industries has taken an initiative for the introduction of Small and Medium Enterprises Development Bill in 2005 which was stabled in Lok Sabha on

Table 2

Production, Employment and Exports in Small Scale Sectors

Year	*No.of Units (in Lakhs)*			*Production (Rs. Crore)*			
	Registered	*Un-registered*	*Total*	*At current prices*	*At 1993-94 prices*	*Employment (lakhs)*	*Export at current Prices (Rs. Crore)*
1994-95**	19.44	6.27	25.71	298,886	266,054	146.56	296,058
1994-95	11.61	67.99	79.60	122,210	109,116	191.40	29,068
1995-96	11.57	71.27	82.84	148,290	121,649	197.93	36,470
1996-97	11.99	74.22	86.21	168,413	135,380	205.86	39,248
1997-98	12.04	77.67	89.71	189,413	147,824	213.16	44,442
1998-99	12.00	81.36	93.36	212,901	159,407	220.50	48,979
1999-00	12.32	84.83	97.15	234,255	170,709	229.10	54,200
2000-01	13.10	88.00	101.10	161,289	184,428	239.09	69,797
2001-02	13.75	91.46	105.10	282,270	195,613	249.09	71,244
2002-03	14.68	95.42	110.10	311,993	210,636	261.38	86,013
2003-04*	15.54	98.41	113.95	357,733	228,730	271.36	NA
2004-05	16.38	102.15	118.53	399,200	245,747	282.82	NA
Average Annual Growth Rate (1994-95 to 2002-03)	3.0	4.3	4.1	12.4	8.6	4.0	14.5

** These figures relate to data given by Ministry of Small Scale Industries earlier.

Source: Ministry of Small Scale Industries as given in Economic Survey (2004-2005) p.156.

12th May. The small industry is being perceived as vital sub-sector of the economy. Small industry generates large employment, removes regional imbalance by contributing to the economic development. However, June 2004 report of the Third All India Census of small scale industries has brought out an alarming picture of the sector. The report highlights the poor performance of small scale industries in some crucial aspects. Units maintaining account books constitute only 9.53 percent. Only 60 percent of the units were using electric power. The employment capability expressed in terms of employment per unit, is only 2.37[14].

Employment in the registered small scale industries sector is estimated at 61.63 lakh, indicating an average employment of 4.48 persons per unit. Besides, 37.47 percent of the total employment was in rural areas. The situation, as it prevailed in 2001-2002, needs to be compared with the much higher level of employment in 1987-88, as documented by the Second Census (6.29 persons).

There is enough evidence to suggest that the globalization era has led to the closure of a large number of units. The percentage of working units declined from 62.75 percent in 1987-88 to 60.77 percent in 2001-2002. Another important finding of the census is a significant move towards service industries from manufacturing activities. The decline in the share of small scale industries, from 96.24 percent to 65.55 percent, and increase in small service business enterprises from 3.24 percent to 34.45 percent, indicates the decline of autonomous enterprises. While nurturing autonomous enterprises was the policy thrust during the pre-liberalization period, the recent growth experience demands major support system for small and medium enterprises. The role of individual units needs a thorough investigation.

The per–unit fixed investment has gone up from Rs. 1.60 lakhs in the second census to Rs. 6.68 lakhs. While this, to some extent, indicates capital–intensity of production, it also implies a decline in the number of labour intensive units. The picture in terms of sources of credit itself indicates the significant informal nature of firms.

The number of units having outstanding loans with institutional sources was only 4.55 percent, which indicates the need for a much greater formalization of production, in order to overcome the challenges thrown up by globalization. Despite all these constraints, per unit investment, employment–investment ratio, and out put–labour ratio, are positive factors which favour small industry.

In a country like India, only a few men with growth perspective would come forward for changing the stationary inertia and creating preconditions for development since they are motivated for higher achievements rather than financial gains. It is impossible to imagine any development process without an entrepreneurial form, not only in capitalistic economy but even under the situation of state capitalism.

The process of development can be visualized with two different types of entrepreneurial activities. The entrepreneurship can emerge either as a result of individual efforts or collective and cooperative efforts. The first type of entrepreneurship is the potent source of development. The experience of India has shown that the public or cooperative techno structures established in a backward region have initiated actively leading to the development of townships but have failed to initiate the process of development in the real terms. In such regions, since the public and cooperative techno structure has its own limitations, it is the local entrepreneurship that must get itself involved in the process of development. The development would not gather momentum if much reliance is placed on the factors beyond local control. Therefore, it is absolutely necessary to break the vicious circle and initiate the process of development. To start with, among others, small–scale entrepreneurship is the most desirable dent.

ANDHRA PRADESH ECONOMY

Andhra Pradesh is the fifth largest state in India both in area and population and it accounts for 8.36 per cent in the total area. The total area of Andhra Pradesh is 2,75,045 sq. km[15] and it is situated in the tropical region between 13° and 20° north of the equator and between 77° and 85° east longitudes. It is bounded by Tamil Nadu (South) Maharashtra (North), Orissa, Madhya Pradesh and Chhattisgarh (North-East), Karnataka (West) and Bay of Bengal (East). The northern area of Andhra Pradesh is having the Krishna and Godavari as the major river systems.

The word 'Andhra' is equally applicable to the land, the people and the language, although the language in course of time developed a name of its own Telugu. Andhra Pradesh is the first state in India that has been formed on a purely linguistic basis. When India became independent, the Andhras, that is, the Telugu speaking people, were distributed in about districts, 9 of them in the Nizam's dominians and 12 in the Madras presidency. On the basis of linguistics, on October 1, 1953, 11 districts of the Madras state were put together to form a new Andhra Pradesh with Kurnool as capital on November 1, 1956 in accordance with the recommendations of the state reorganization commission. The Andhra State was enlarged by the addition of nine districts formerly in the Nizam's dominion. Hyderabad, the former capital of the Nizam, was made the capital of the enlarged Andhra State. On April 1, 1960, 573.43 sq. km in the Chengleput and Salem districts of Madras were transferred to Andhra Pradesh in exchange for 1062 sq. km from Chittoor District. The district of Prakasam was formed on February 2, 1970. Hyderabad was split into two districts on August 15, 1978 a new district, Vijayaanagaram, was formed in 1979 the 23 districts of the state fall into three natural regions. East Godavari, Guntur, Krishna, Nellore, Prakasam, Srikakulam, Visakhapatnam, Vijayanagaram and West Godavari districts constitute, Andhra region, Adilabad, Hyderabad, Kareemnagar, Khammam, Mahaboob Nagar, Medak, Nalgonda, Nizamabad and Warangal districts are in the Telengana Region and Chittoor, Cuddapah, Kurnool, and Ananthapur constitute the Rayalaseema region[16].

The state has abundant mineral wealth and it accounts for about 98 % of copper ore. In respect of manganese ore production, the state ranks sixth in the country. It also ranks second in respect of mica and limestone production. The famous Singareni coal mines supply coal to the entire South India.

With a 970 km coastline, Andhra Pradesh is a major maritime state in India. Visakhapatnam is the major port while Kakinada, Machilipatnam, Bheemunipatnam, Krishnapatnam, Vodarevu and Kalingapatnam are the minor ports. Important airports are located in Hyderabad, Tirupathi, Vijayawada and Visakhapatnam.

Hyderabad and Visakhapatnam are the main centres of major industries. They are known for the production of machine tools, synthetic drugs, pharmaceuticals, heavy electrical machinery, ships, fertilizers, electric equipment, aeronautical parts, cement, chemicals, asbestos and glass. Hyderabad once known as a pharma city emerging quickly as a hub of information technology. Major IT Corporations are coming to Andhra Pradesh. World Major IT companies like Infosysis Technologies, Microsoft USA, Wipro, International Business Machine (IBM), Cognizant Technologies etc., are coming to Hyderabad which has become a preferred designation after Bangalore and Chennai.

The state ranks fourth in industrial investments with public sector undertakings include Bharath Heavy Electrical Limited, Indian Drugs and Pharmaceuticals Limited, Hindustan Aeronautical Limited, Bharath Dynamic Limited, Bharath Heavy Plates and Vessels, Vizag Steel Plant and Electronic Corporation of India Limited. During the 8th plan, the state generated 1296 mw of additional power taking the total power generation of 7276 mw. Private sector participation is being sought to double this by the 9th Plan that end. It is hoped that Andhra Pradesh will have surplus power by 2010, with availability of more than 1000 mw from National Thermal Power Corporation, 220 mw from the private sector and 900 mw from Srisailam. Important power projects in Andhra Pradesh are : Machkund, Upper Sileru, Lower

Sileru, Tungabadra Dam, Nagarjuna Sagar, Sri Sailam, and Nizam Sagar, Hydel Power Schemes and Nellore, Ramagundam, Kothagudem and Vijayawada thermal stations. Power sector reforms in Andhra Pradesh have motivated many entrepreneurs like G.V.K. Group, G.M.R. Vasavi group, Lanco etc to set up their gas-based power plants particularly in and around Krishna-Godavari basin where natural gas is available.

There are 2,999 large and medium scale industries in the State with a total investment of Rs. 41,077 crores, providing employment to 8,02,209 persons as on 31 March 2001, the number of tiny and small scale industries were 3,29,444 with credit assistance of Rs.2,707.53 crores and employing 28,09,468 persons. National highways in Andhra Pradesh are 3967km and state highways cover 60,982 km. There are 100,468 km of Panchayati roads. Railway routes cover 5,029 km[17]. Work is in full swing in India's first underground hydel station being set up in a space created underneath the hills on the left bank of the Sri Sailam Project.

NELLORE DISTRICT ECONOMY

Nellore is a place of great antiquity. A king by name VIKRAM SIMHAPURI ruled Nellore. After his death, this town name was denoted as Nellore. Thus the earliest name for Nellore was to be 'SIMHAPURI'. The district lies between 13-30' and 15-6' of the Northern Latitude & 70-5' and 80-15' of the Eastern Longitude and extending over an area of 13076 Sq. kms, accounting for 4.75% of the total area of the state. It is bounded on the North by Prakasam district on the East by Bay of Bengal on the South by Chittoor district and Chengalpattu district of Tamil Nadu and on the West by Veligonda Hills which separate it from Cuddapah district[18]. Administratively the district is divided into 46 mandals, covering three revenue divisions with head quarters in Nellore, Gudur and Kavali. There are three municipalities namely Venkatagiri, Gudur and Kavali and in addition there are two census towns i.e., Kovurpalli, Venkatagiri.

As per 2001 Census, the total population of the district is 26.68 Lakhs. Out of which male population is 13.45 lakhs and female population is 13.23 lakhs. The rural population is 20.69 lakhs and urban population is 5.99 lakhs. The population of females per 1000 male is 984[19]. The total literacy population in the district is 15.23 lakhs covering 65.08% of the total population in the district. Out of which, male literates are 8.67 lakhs covering 73.67% and female literates are 6.56 lakhs covering 56.38%.

The district has 222 km length of broad gauge lines having 27 railways stations. Out of the 46 mandals, 12 mandals have the facility of railway stations. In respect of road lines national highway of 194 km length of roads whereas, state highways cover 759 kms length of roads. All mandals in the district are well connected with pucca roads having good frequency of bus facility.

Agriculture is the main occupation of the people of the district. The total cropped area in the district is 3.07 lakh hectares during the year 2003-2004. Out of which Paddy (1.55 lakh hectares), sugarcane (0.11 lakh hectares), Groundnut (0.14 hectares), Cotton (0.10 lakh hectares), Black gram (0.47 lakh hectares), Tobacco (0.10 lakh hectares) etc., are main crops. In addition, horticulture produces like mango, banana, guava and lime are grown. Recently growth of aqua culture has predominantly made majority of agriculturists to convert their agricultural fields into ponds to cultivate prawns taking advantage of long coastal line. This has resulted in the growth of aqua-culture and aqua-exports.

Nellore district is also rich in other minerals like quartz, silica sand lime shell, lime stone, barytes, copper ore, vermicule, chinaclay, etc., Deposits of quartz with 98% of silica are found in Rapur, Gudur and Chagnam villages. Deposits of lime are found along the banks of Pulicat Lake. Limestones of gray and pink colour are found in Vinjamur.

The district has coastal line of 169 kms covering 12 mandals. There are 93 crores of fishermen habitations having 82500 populations out of which 16300 are active fishermen. The estimated marine landings in the district are 54941 mts. There is a Pulicat lake which is the second biggest brackish water lake in the country with an area of 468 sq.kms. The lake accounts for annual production of 6500 mts of Fishery wealth providing livelihood to 11000 fisherman covering 20 kuppams around the lake.

The district has good infrastructure for primary; higher and professional education. It has eight engineering colleges, one medical and dental College, besides a large number of primary schools and degree colleges. The people of the district are known to be industrious and entrepreneurial. Nellore is well known for entrepreneurship in coaching education throughout the country like Narayana Coaching Centre, Rathnam coaching institute etc.,

The coastal district of Nellore is located along the Bay of Bengal coast. The district is also known for the entrepreneurial spirit generally found among its people. The district has wide network of banking facilities. The district has 139 Commercial Bank branches, 56 grameena bank branches (Pinakini Grameena Bank) and 15 branches of Nellore District Co–operative Central Bank branches and a branch of Andhra Pradesh State Financial Corporation. 62 % of bank branches are in rural areas and 38 % of bank branches in semi urban/urban areas, the total deposits of the bank for the district as a whole are Rs. 1030.15 crores and advances outstanding Rs. 856.22 crores[20].

Many entrepreneurs from Nellore district have successfully established hotels and catering services spread in various cities and towns of South India. The industrial development, infrastructure and business in Nellore district are comparable.

The Nellore district is one of the industrially backward districts of the state of Andhra Pradesh placed under the 'C' category by the Central Government for the purpose of determining the eligibility of subsidy for new investments in the district. Inspite of its proximity to the industrial belt of Chennai and availability of railway heads, 180 kms of national highways, power etc., the district has lagged behind in industrial development. At present, 35 large and medium scale Industries are working in the district with an investment of Rs. 758.11 crores and 7298 workers are employed.

Nellore district is potentially a good district for the development of tiny and small scale units. There has been a constant increase in the establishment of small scale enterprises over the last decade. 20978 small scale industries[21] are working with capital investment Rs. 261.09 crores and 94541 workers are working in these industries as per the Table 3.

Table 3

Categorywise Classification of Small Scale Industries As On 31-3-04

Category	*No. of Units*	*Capital Investment (Rs.lakhs)*	*Employment*
Textile based	1866	952.44	648
Mineral based	222	614.93	1890
Forest based	2069	2268.51	8218
Leather & Footwear	38	24.22	130
Food & Agro based	2636	5456.12	15720
Engineering based	2589	4473.85	9888
Chemical	916	2283.16	6437
Building Materials	1450	2543.97	13101
Electronics	623	348.85	2145
Plastics & Rubber	1240	997.65	3842
Paper & Board	39	401.75	283
Printing	23	124.64	150
Miscellaneous	7258	5619.05	32090
Total	20978	26109.14	94541

Source: Records of District Industries Centres, Nellore, 2004.

The Nellore district has nine industrial estates of which four are in Nellore Corporation i.e., Andhra Pradesh Private Industrial Estate, Wood Complex, Autonagar Phase I & Autonagar Phase II and others are Industrial Estate, Gudur; Industrial Estate, Kavali; Industrial Developing Areas, Pannemgadu; Integrated Industries

Development Centre, Tada and Industrial Developing Area, Venkatachalam.

Total number of industrial sheds constructed is 48, of which 42 are in Nellore Corporation (Auto Nagar PH_2). Besides, there are 1207 industrial plots developed by Andhra Pradesh Industrial Infrastructural Corporation (APIIC). The Table 4 indicates the details regarding plots, sheds, geographical area covered and working units of Industrial Developing Area (IDA)/Industrial Estate (IE) in Nellore district.

Table 4
Industrial Estates: Sheds, Plots, Geographical Area Covered and Working Units

	Estate of land (in acres)		*Total No.of Plots*	*Total No.of Sheds*	*No. of Units Working*
Name of the Estate	*Acquired*	*Developed*			
APIE, Nellore	33.28	33.28	97	-	60
Wood Complex, Nellore	51.95	51.95	103	-	101
Autonagar PH1, Nellore	36.68	36.68	250	-	210
Autonagar PH2, Nellore	60.74	60.74	360	42	212
Industrial Estate, Gudur	26.47	26.47	22	6	19
Industrial Estate, Kavali	29.50	29.50	40	-	24
IDA, Pannemgedu	24.24	24.24	38	-	22
IIDc, Tada	108.00	108.00	151	-	5
IDA, Venkatachalam	67.03	67.03	146	-	-

Source: Records of APIIC, Nellore, 2004.

Main regions of Nellore Corporation like Andhra Pradesh Industrial Estate, Wood Complex, Autonagar PH 1 and Autonagar PH 2 have more number of working units. Autonagar PH 2 of Nellore Corporation which has the highest number of units 212, out of 360 plots and 42 sheds. Industrial Estate of Gudur, Kavali and Pannemgedu have 19, 24, 22 units. IIDc , Tada having lowest number of units i.e., five. IDA, Venkatachalam only plots were developed but units are not yet started. It is due to nonavailabity of raw materials, lack of proper marketing facilities and competition from entrepreneurs of Chennai city. Entrepreneurs prefer to have enterprise in urban area than in rural Tada. The entrepreneurs of the urban area are satisfied with IE/IDA than rural. This is because of the sites located in villages, do not have transport and water facilities.

The people of the district are better educated and comparatively have shown higher drive and entrepreneurial competencies for setting up small enterprises. The communication network in the district is very good.

According to District Industries Centre, scope for industrial development has been found in sectors such as tourism, software development and bio technology industries.

STUDY REGION

The study is concerned with the growth and development of entrepreneurship in the Nellore district. The Nellore district was chosen for the study, as the growth of small enterprises has significant scope. Further, the researchers own interest with small enterprises was another motivating factor for the selection of study region. The study of motivational region dealing with the enterprise and nature of problems faced by small enterprises was of specific interest to the researcher for the academic purpose.

SUMMARY

In summary, the Nellore district was selected as the study area. The industrial infrastructure, natural resources, human resources and entrepreneurial drive of the people of the district are the key factors for accelerated growth of small enterprises. Most of the modern small enterprises were established in developed sheds/ industrial areas of this region. The study of small enterprises in Nellore, Gudur and Kavali region would form the representative sample of similar units in the Nellore district. The determinants of Growth and Development of Entrepreneurship are analyzed in the following chapter.

REFERENCES

1. Census of India (2001), Office of Registrar General & Census Commissioner, Series I, India, p.4
2. *Ibid.*
3. Ruddar Datt and Sundharam K.P.M. (2006), "Indian Economy", S. Chand and Company Ltd., New Delhi, p.646-650.
4. Government of India (2003), Economic Survey, 2002-2003, Statement 2.7, New Delhi, p.S-41.
5. Government of India (1999), Planning Commission, Ninth Five Year Plan, 1997-2002, Vol.II, New Delhi, p.3 and 595-600.
6. Government of India (2003), Planning Commission, Tenth Five Year Plan, 2002-2007, Vol.I, Annexure.3-A, New Delhi, p.87.
7. Tenth Five Year Plan, op.cit., Vol.II, p.665.
8. Sudip Chaudhuri (2002), "Economic Reforms and Industrial Structure in India", Economic and Political Weekly, January 12th, Table 3, p.157 and 160.
9. Nagaraj. R. (2002), "Performance of India's Manufacturing Sector in the 1990s: Some Tentative Findings", Shuji Uchikawa (ed.,), Economic Reforms and Industrial Structure in India, Delhi, p.19
10. *Ibid,* Table.3, p.18.
11. Government of India, Planning Commission, Fourth Five Year Plan, 1969-74, Vol.II,.p.21-22.
12. Government of India (1999), Planning Commission, Ninth Five Year Plan, 1997-2002, Vol.II, Delhi, p.604.
13. Ruddar Datt and Sundharam , K.P.M, op.cit., p.690.
14. Mathew, P.W. (2005), "SME Package: Lingering Lacunae", The Hindu, August 15th, p.15.
15. Andhra Pradesh Year Book (2004), 2003-2004, Government of Andhra Pradesh, Vol.I, Hyderabad, p.12.
16. *Ibid.*
17. Andhra Pradesh Year Book (2004), 2003-2004, Government of Andhra Pradesh, Vol.II, Hyderabad, p.260
18. Hand Book of Statistics (2004), Chief Planning Officer, Nellore, p.3

19. *Ibid*, p.1.
20. Service Area Credit Plan (2005), Syndicate Bank, Lead District Office, Nellore, p.4.
21. Annual Report (2004), Andhra Pradesh Industrial Infrastructural Corporation, Nellore, p.16.

5

DETERMINANTS OF GROWTH & DEVELOPMENT OF ENTREPRENEURSHIP

INTRODUCTION

Having outlined the socio-economic profile of the study region in which the entrepreneurs under study are operating, in the previous chapter, now it is appropriate to turn to the entrepreneurs themselves.

This chapter presents the analysis and interpretation of data collected from the 196 respondent units focusing on specific issues related to growth and development of entrepreneurship. The data is analyzed and presented in various sections. The various sections elicited information on socio– economic profile of the entrepreneurs, motivating factors, growth factors i.e., investment, human resource, marketing and profitability, current problems faced, impact of globalization and liberalization and opinions on entrepreneurial success.

SOCIO–ECONOMIC BACKGROUND OF RESPONDENTS

It is proposed to identify the sources of small scale entrepreneurship in Nellore district by their socio-economic characteristics–caste, age, educational level, family background, form of organization etc. The entrepreneurial activity at any time is dependent on a complex and varying mixture of socio-economic, psychological and other factors. Thus a multitude of factors affect entrepreneurial spirit among people and they, in turn cast their influence on environment. The process of interaction and adaptation between the individual and his environment goes on. At any given moment of time, the individuals take meanings from the situations in which they find themselves through the media of social roles, group norms and cultures, past experiences and future expectations[1].

The period after Independence has witnessed tremendous economic, social and political changes in India. These changes had their profound influence on entrepreneurial activity in different regions of the country. Several new entrepreneurial communities not known for mercantile background, traditionally came forward to start economic activities in trade, manufacturing and service sectors. Their scale of operation is generally small. And the small business is a key element in the operation of Indian economy and it will continue to be so in the foreseeable future. Hence, an analysis of factors which prompted 196 such entrepreneurs chosen for this study (operating in Nellore district) who made a dent in business before and after Independence may provide a clue to the influences to which these new and small entrepreneurs reacted to.

Form of Ownership

The form of ownership was presented in the Figure 1.

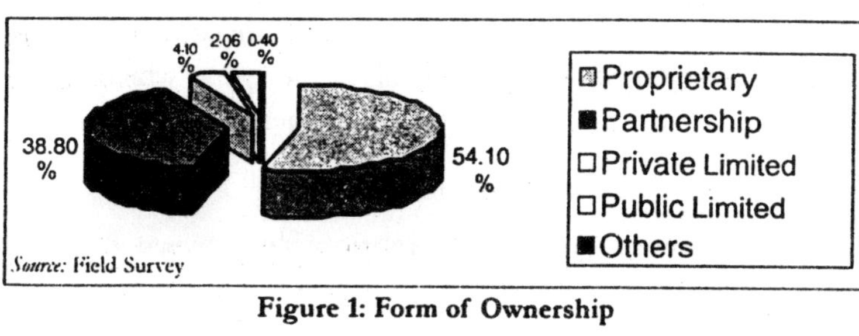

Figure 1: Form of Ownership

Proprietary type of organization was the prominent type (54.1 percent), followed by partnership type (38.8 percent). Together these two types accounted for 92.9 percent. Public limited companies were only five in number (2.6 percent).

The types of organizational set up of the small enterprises were mostly proprietary, partnership, private limited and public limited to a very small extent. In proprietary type of organizations, the owner–manager was the sole proprietor. Therefore, the owner–manager in such organization usually has to attend to all the managerial and routine operational tasks single handed.

Age of the Entrepreneur

An attempt has been made to ascertain the age of the entrepreneurs and is presented in the below Table.

Table 1
Age of the Entrepreneur

Entrepreneur's Age (in Years)	*No. of Entrepreneurs*	*Percentage*
Below & 25 years 2.	26-353.	36-504.
Above 50	2888728	14.344.936.7 4.1
Total	196	100.00

Mean =32.96, Median=32.95, Mode=32.89, SD=66.71.
Source: Field Survey

The Table 1 shows the age of the entrepreneurs of which 14.3 percent of promoter's age was below 25 years, 44.9 percent of them in the age group of 26-35 years and 36.7 percent were in the age group of 36-50 years. The mean age was 32.96 years and the standard deviation was 66.71.

Thus it is healthy sign that young people are coming forward to start their own enterprises and this is the age at which one is full of vigour and enthusiasm to start business of their own.

Age and Form of Ownership

The Table below shows the cross relationship between the form of ownership and age of the entrepreneurs.

Table 2
Age and Form of Ownership

Form of Ownership	*Age of the Entrepreneurs*									
	Below & 25 years		26-35 years		36-50 years		Above 50 years		Total	
	No	%	No	%	No	%	No	%	No	%
Proprietary	23(21.7)	82.14	40(37.7)	45.45	39(36.7)	54.16	4(3.7)	50	106(100)	54.08
Partnership	5(6.6)	17.86	40(52.7)	45.45	28(36.8)	38.88	3(3.9)	37.5	76(100)	38.77
Private Ltd	-	-	8(100)	9.10	-	-	-	-	8(100)	4.08
Public Ltd	-	-	-	-	4(80)	5.58	1(20)	12.5	5(100)	2.55
Others	-	-	-	-	1(100)	1.38	-	-	1(100)	0.52
Total	28	100	88	100	72	100	8	100	196	100

Note : Figures in parentheses represent percentages
The calculated value of chi-square =11.52
Table value of chi-square at 0.01 percent level=10.60

Source: Field Survey

The above Table shows that 82.14 percent of the respondents whose age below 25 years were sole proprietors followed by the respondents (54.16) whose age was between 36-50 years were also running the propriety concerns. On the other hand 52.7 percent of the respondents whose age was between 26-35 were partners of their enterprise.

The chi-square test, revealed a computed value of (11.52) which is higher than the theoretical value (10.60) at 0.01 percent level with two degrees of freedom. It indicates that there is a significant association between the form of organisation and the age of the entrepreneurs. This may be due to the fact that many small scale enterprises across the country were owned by sole proprietors.

Educational Level

Economists have long been aware of the importance of education in the development of human resources[2]. If one rejects the notion that investment in education must be productive, then he should also be prepared to reject the goal of rapid economic progress[3].

.However, learning neither begins nor ends in schools or colleges. It is a continuous process. Leaning gives the learners a feeling of self–realization or resourceful what Nayudamma calls[4]. Self realization brings out the potential resourcefulness which in turn leads to self confidence, self control and thus makes one more skilful in solving problems. All learning is to make a living. But education is more than that. It is for better living, fullness of living and more important, to be responsive to the society. Education should bring out the best from the man and thus aid the development of a nation. Development of a nation is the development of man. Man means his resourcefulness. Resourcefulness means initiative and enterprise to find new and better ways and initiative to look for group opportunities and turn them into realizations. This is how education, entrepreneurship and development are interrelated, and education is the best source of developing man's resourcefulness. In essence, the resourcefulness covers all the aspects and embraces all the dimensions of entrepreneurship. Education is not for "relief" but for "release" of potential resourcefulness in man. Education is not to make people wealthy but productive, to make people an asset and not a liability. As such, in a developing economy with egalitarian objectives, the environment for entrepreneurship should not depend upon hereditary factors, the educational system should give the necessary base in order to equip the child to benefit from entrepreneurial opportunities in his career[5].

Thus formal education is always considered an important asset of an individual in building occupational career in a bureaucratic society. Therefore, in developing economy, education is always looked upon as a means to improve one's socio-economic status of the society. The formal education is expected to increase the supply of entrepreneurs by making available more skills necessary to entrepreneurial endeavour. But, in an underdeveloped economy, the educated are likely to take up positions in the bureaucracy as it commands more respect in the society and also generates assured income[6].

It is proposed to ascertain the educational level of the entrepreneurs. The results are as follows.

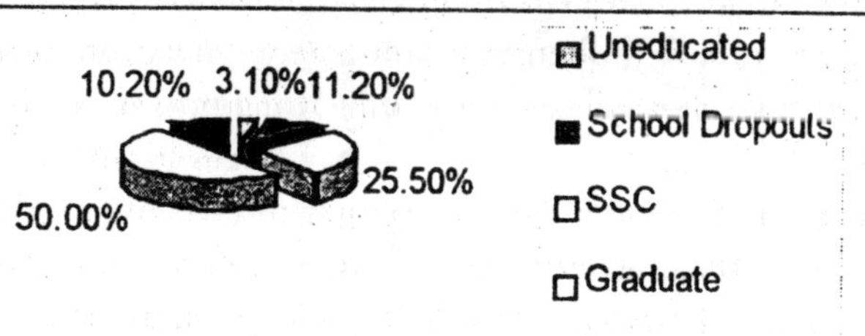

*SSC – Secondary School Certificate
Source: Field Survey

Figure 2: Educational Qualifications of the Respondents

The respondents without any formal education are kept under uneducated category. The respondents who had been to the school and discontinued are included as school drops.

Table 3

Educational Qualification and Form of Ownership

Form of Ownership	Educational Qualifications of the Entrepreneurs										Total	
	Uneducated		School Dropouts		SSC		Graduate		PG & above			
	No	%	No	%	No	%	No	%	No	%	No	%
Proprietary	3(2.8)	50	14(13.4)	63.63	21(19.8)	42	57(53.7)	58.2	11(10.3)	55	106(100)	54.08
Partnership	3(3.9)	50	4(5.3)	18.2	26(34.3)	52	34(44.7)	34.7	9(11.8)	45	76(100)	38.77
Private Ltd	-	-	1(12.5)	4.54	2(25)	4	5(62.5)	5.1	-	-	8(100)	4.08
Public Ltd	-	-	2(40)	9.09	1(100)	2	2(40)	2.05	-	-	5(100)	2.55
Others	-	-	1(100)	4.54	-	-	-	-	-	-	1(100)	0.52
Total	6	100	22	100	50	100	98	100	20	100	196	100

Note: Figures in parentheses represent percentages
The calculated value of chi-square = 4.10
Table value of chi-square at 0.05 percent level=9.35

Source: Field Survey

Education-wise, degree holders form the major section of respondents constituting 50 percent of the total. As the sample units were modern small enterprises, majority of the promoters had college education.

Educational Qualification and Form of Ownership

The following Table 3 shows the distribution of respondents on the basis of educational qualification and form of ownership.

It is seen in the above Table 3 that the 53.7 percentage of respondents who are graduates and sole proprietors of their enterprise. On the other hand 5.3 percent respondents who completed school education are partners of their enterprise.

The chi-square test, however found that form of ownership and educational qualifications of entrepreneurs are independent of one another. The calculated value of chi-square with three degree of freedom (4.10) is found to be less than the theoretical value at 0.05 percent level (9.35) and therefore, it is concluded that there is hardly any association between these two variables.

Educational Qualification and Age of the Entrepreneurs

The following Table 4 shows the distribution of respondents on the basis of educational qualification and age of the entrepreneurs.

From the tabulated data, it is evident that 71.4 percent of the respondents having graduation were below 25 years. Further, 2.8 percent of respondents who were uneducated were in the age group of 36-50 years.

The value of chi-square clearly shows that there were significant association between educational qualification and age of the entrepreneurs. The calculated value of chi-square (9.06) is found to be greater than the theoretical value (7.38) at 0.05 percent level with two degrees of freedom and it may be concluded that young graduates were coming towards entrepreneurship.

Educational Qualification and Gender of the Entrepreneur

The details about respondents' educational qualifications and gender are presented in the following Table 5.

Table 4
Educational Qualification and Age of the Entrepreneurs

Age	Uneducated		School Dropout		SSC		Graduate		PG & above		Total	
	No	%	No	%	No	%	No	%	No	%	No	%
Below &25 yrs	-	-	3(10.8)	13.63	4(14.2)	8	20(71.4)	20.4	1(3.6)	5	28(100)	14.28
26-35 yrs	3(3.4)	50	12(13.6)	54.54	30(34.1)	60	39(44.3)	39.79	4(4.6)	20	88(100)	44.89
36-50 yrs	2(2.8)	33.33	5(6.9)	22.72	15(20.8)	30	36(50)	36.73	14(19.5)	70	72(100)	36.73
Above 50 yrs	1(12.5)	16.64	2(25)	9.11	1(12.5)	2	3(37.5)	3.08	1(12.5)	5	8(100)	4.01
Total	6	100	22	100	50	100	98	100	20	100	196	100

Note: Figures in parentheses represent percentages
The calculated value of chi-square = 9.06
Table value of chi-square at 0.05 percent level=7.38

Source: Field Survey

Table 5

Educational Qualification and Gender of the Entrepreneur

Gender	*Educational Qualifications of the Entrepreneurs*											
	Uneducated		*School Dropout*		*SSC*		*Graduate*		*PG & above*		*Total*	
	No	*%*	*No*	*%*	*No*	*%*	*No*	*%*	*No*	*%*	*No*	*%*
Male	5(3.6)	83.33	15(10.6)	68.18	41(28.6)	82	70(48.9)	71.42	12(8.3)	60	143(100)	72.95
Female	1(1.8)	16.64	7(13.2)	31.82	9(17)	18	28(53)	28.58	8(15)	40	53(100)	27.05
Total	6	100	22	100	50	100	98	100	20	100	196	100

Note: Figures in parentheses represent percentages
The calculated value of chi-square =3.92
Table value of chi-square at 0.01 percent level=14.4

Source: Field Survey

The information presented in the Table clearly shows that about 48.9 percent of the respondents were males with graduate degree, similarly 53 percent of the respondents were females' graduates.

The calculated value of chi-square (3.92) at six degree of freedom is less than the theoretical distribution (14.4) at 0.05 percent level signifying that no such association existed between these variables. It leads to the conclusion that majority of entrepreneurs were graduates irrespective of their sex.

Caste of the Entrepreneur

The social base of entrepreneurship is an important factor influencing the pace of economic development. If certain social groups alone produce a large and capable body of entrepreneurs, the means for such impetus may be relevance and use to the entire society. This view was upheld by Everett Hagen[7] in his studies of the origin and background of entrepreneurs of several countries and regions, including England, Western Soviet Union, Japan and Latin America. In several countries, entrepreneurs have emerged from a particular socio-economic class. In Britain, United States of America and Turkey, the ranks of entrepreneurs were filled from commerce[8]. It has often been suggested that certain religions encourage the growth of entrepreneurial ability. The protestant ethic of the West was considered to have significantly contributed to the emergence of a new class of industrialists. In Japan, it was the Sanurai who turned to industry and kept their social structure intact through marriage[9]. The emergence of smaller firms in France was attributed to the social structure, especially to their family pattern[10]. Mc Clelland also found that many of the pockets of poverty in the U.S.A were due to the scarcity of well motivated entrepreneurs.

A review of literature on entrepreneurship in less developed economies indicates that the entrepreneurship is confined to a few groups or communities. For instance in Nigeria, the Yoruba and Ibo tribes have always had a much greater achievement motivation than the Hausa and Fulani[11]. In Kenya, the Kikuyu displayed the entrepreneurial spirit, while in South East Asia, the Chinese, and to a lesser extent the Indians, were risk takers[12]. In Lebanon, Christians constituted a high proportion of entrepreneurs as compared to their half of the share in population. Only one-sixth of the entrepreneurial groups were Muslims compared to their share of 44 percent in total population[13] In Philippines, impressive amount of mobility was noticed among the entrepreneurs[14]. Greek industrialists represented Greek refugees resulting from the exchange of minorities between Turkey and Greece[15]. Pakistani industrialists were well represented by Muslim members of Halai Memon, Chinioti, Dawoodi Bohra, Khoja Ismali and Khoja Isnasharai communities[16]

The history of growth of entrepreneurship in India leaves many questions unanswered. Why people only from certain communities[17] were attracted to entrepreneurship? Why did not the spirit of enterprise permeate among other sections of the society? Again why did it concentrate on a few families even among business communities? The expansion for the absence of broad based entrepreneurship in India is commonly found in the caste system, the joint family living and the social and cultural values associated with them.

The Indian entrepreneurship has always been discussed and analysed in terms of entrepreneurs' caste and the pursuits associated with caste. The caste system has had to some extent, its effect on occupational mobility. The caste factor has to be considered while studying the entrepreneurship as the latter prefers a particular culture imbibed from certain castes. In India, some religious communities like the Parsis, Marwais and Sindhees have an affinity for industrial activity[18]. Several studies undertaken at the regional level showed predominance of certain communities among the entrepreneurial classes.

An attempt has been made to ascertain the caste of the entrepreneurs. The sample may be said to be quite representative in the sense that the entrepreneurs covered under the study were of forward caste, backward caste, scheduled caste and scheduled tribe as is shown in the Figure below.

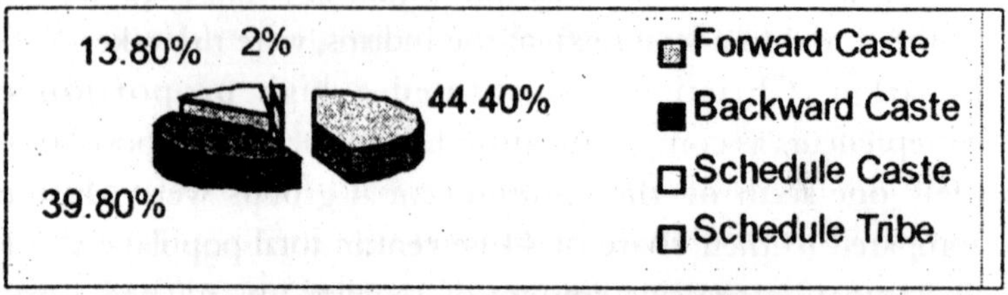

Figure 3: Caste of the Entrepreneurs

Source: Field Survey

Note: All those castes did not come under notified list of backward class, scheduled caste and scheduled tribes are treated as forward caste.

From the above Figure, it is clear that of the 196 entrepreneurs 87 (44.4%) were of forward caste, 78 (39.8%) were of backward caste, 27 (13.8%) were of scheduled caste and remaining 4 (2.0%) were scheduled tribe. Since entrepreneurs of forward caste form the majority of Indian entrepreneurial population and their numbers is quite commensurate with the population composition of backward caste are also leading in business and industry. Though they are in minority yet their participation in business and industry is appreciable. Entrepreneurship among scheduled caste and scheduled tribe is very poor. Besides, as many as 31 (15.8%) entrepreneurs belonged to scheduled caste and scheduled tribe. It testifies to the fact that scheduled caste and schedule tribe are no more cut off from the main stream of India's economic development. They are equally contributing to the economy of our country.

Family Background

The promoter father's occupations were noted in the Table 6a. It was observed that 38.8 percent of them belonged to agriculture, 33.7 percent to business, 26.5 percent in employment and remaining 1 percent belong to professional/others services. Only 33.7 percent of them belonged to business families engaged in manufacturing or service industries.

Table 6a
Occupation of the Entrepreneur's Father

Father's Occupation	*No of Entrepreneurs*	*Percentage*
Agriculture	76	38.8
Business	66	33.7
Government Employee	52	26.5
Professional	2	1
Total	196	100.0

Source: Field Survey

It could be inferred that two thirds of entrepreneurs were first generation entrepreneurs.

Table 6b
Educational Qualifications of the Entrepreneur's Father

Father's Education	*No of Entrepreneurs*	*Percentage*
Uneducated	45	23.0
School Dropouts	78	39.8
SSC	63	32.1
Graduate	10	5.1
Total	196	100.0

Source: Field Survey

The educational qualifications of the respondent's father were noted in the Table 6b. It was observed that 39.8 percent were school dropouts, 32.1 percent were SSC, 23 percent were uneducated, and 10 percent were graduates. Together, 62.8 percent of the respondent's fathers are not having basic education.

It could be seen from the above Table 6b that educational level of respondents and their fathers' literacy level have been increasing over the generations.

Educational Qualification and Caste of the Entrepreneurs

The distribution of the respondents on the basis of the educational qualification and caste is presented in the Table given below.

Table 7
Educational Qualification and Caste of the Entrepreneurs

	Educational Qualifications of the Entrepreneurs											
	Uneducated		*School Dropout*		*SSC*		*Graduate*		*PG & above*		*Total*	
Caste of the Entrepreneurs	*No*	*%*	*No*	*%*	*No*	*%*	*No*	*%*	*No*	*%*	*No*	*%*
ForwardCaste	2(2.4)	33.34	11(12.6)	50	21(24.2)	42	46(52.8)	46.9	7(8)	35	87(100)	44.38
Backward Caste	-	-	8(10.3)	36.36	17(21.8)	34	40(51.3)	40.8	13(16.6)	65	78(100)	39.79
Schedule Caste	4(14.9)	66.66	3(11.1)	13.63	10(37)	20	10(37)	10.2	-		27(100)	13.77
Schedule Tripe	-	-	-	-	2(50)	4	2(50)	2.04	-		4(100)	2.06
Total	6	100	22	100	50	100	98	100	20	100	196	100

Note: Figures in parentheses represent percentages
The calculated value of chi-square =8.17
Table value of chi-square at 0.05 percent level=7.38

Source: Field Survey

Out of 98 graduates, 46.93 percent belonged to forward caste, 40.81 percent are backward caste and scheduled castes are 10.22 percent. The percentage of scheduled tribe are insignificant 2.0 percent and the chi-square test of computed value (8.17) is higher than that the theoretical value (7.38) at 0.05 percent level with the two degrees of freedom, which thereby permits a safe inference that the forward caste and graduate entrepreneurs were preferring to take up entrepreneurial activity. It leads to a conclusion that the Government Reservation Policy failed to promote the scheduled caste and scheduled tribe to go for higher education and for entrepreneurial activity.

Form of the Ownership and Caste of the Entrepreneurs

The distribution of respondents on the basis of form of ownership and caste of the entrepreneurs has been presented in the following Table 8.

It is clear from the Table 8 that about 47.3 percent of entrepreneurs of forward caste were the owners of proprietary concern. On the other hand 40.8 percent of the backward caste own partnership firms.

It is evident from the Table 8 that there is hardly any relationship between the form of ownership and caste of the entrepreneur. The calculated value of chi-square with two degree of freedom (0.88) is found to be less than the theoretical value at 0.05 percent level (7.38) strengthens the above argument. It is clear that entering into a partnership is, by and large, a result of economic compulsions.

Caste and Age of the Entrepreneurs

The distribution of respondents on the basis of caste and age has been presented in the following Table 9.

It is seen that a 42.52 percent of the respondents having forward caste were age group between 26 and 35 years. Similarly, backward caste, (43.58 percent), scheduled caste (51.85 percent),

Table 8
Form of Ownership and Caste wise Distribution

Form of Ownership	Caste of the Entrepreneurs									
	Forward Caste		Backward Caste		Schedule Caste		Schedule Tribe		Total	
	No	%	No	%	No	%	No	%	No	%
Proprietary	50(47.3)	57.47	41(38.6)	52.56	14(13.2)	51.85	1(0.9)	25	106(100)	54.10
Partnership	34(44.8)	39.10	31(40.8)	39.74	9(11.8)	33.33	2(2.6)	50	76(100)	38.77
Private Ltd	1(12.)	1.14	4(50)	5.14	2(25)	7.4	1(12.5)	25	8(100)	4.08
Public Ltd	2(40)	2.19	1(20)	1.28	2(40)	7.4	-	-	5(100)	2.55
Others	-	-	1(100)	1.28	-	-	-	-	1(100)	0.5
Total	87	100	78	100	27	100	4	100	196	100

Note: Figures in parentheses represent percentages
The calculated value of chi-square =0.88
Table value of chi-square at 0.05 percent level=7.38

Source: Field Survey

Table 9
Caste and Age of the Entrepreneurs

Age of the Entrepreneurs	*Caste of the Entrepreneurs*									
	Forward Caste		*Backward Caste*		*Schedule Caste*		*Schedule Tribe*		*Total*	
	No	*%*	*No*	*%*	*No*	*%*	*No*	*%*	*No*	*%*
Below &25 yrs	20(71.4)	22.98	5(17.9)	6.42	3(10.7)	11.11	-	-	28(100)	14.28
26-35 yrs	37(42)	42.52	34(38.6)	43.58	14(16)	51.85	3(3.4)	75	88(100)	44.89
36-50 yrs	27(37.5)	31.03	34(47.2)	43.58	10(13.9)	37.04	1(1.4)	25	72(100)	36.73
Above 50 yrs	3(37.5)	3.47	5(62.5)	6.42			-	-	8(100)	4.10
Total	87	100	78	100	27	100	4	100	196	100

Note: Figures in parentheses represent percentages
The calculated value of chi-square =10.03
Table value of chi-square at 0.05 percent level=7.38

Source: Field Survey

scheduled tribe (75 percent) were also of age group between 26 and 35 years.

The calculated value of chi-square (10.03) is found to be greater than the theoretical value (7.38) at 0.05 percent level with two degrees of freedom. This indicates that there is a significant association between age and caste of entrepreneurs.

Caste and Gender of the Entrepreneurs

The following Table 10 shows the distribution of respondents on the basis of caste and gender of the entrepreneurs.

From the tabulated data, it is evident that large proportions (83.90 percent) of respondents having forward caste were males. On the other hand 35.90 percent of female respondents belonged to the backward classes.

The chi-square test, however found that gender and caste are independent of one another. The calculated value of chi-square with four degree of freedom (9.51) is found to be less than the theoretical value (11.10) at 0.05 percent level. It is heartening to note that the good number of women from less privileged caste were motivated to start the enterprises of their own along with men.

Economic Status

Metaphorically, finance is the life giving element in the process of economic growth. Financial soundness of the entrepreneurs and their elders is supposed to stimulate the growth of entrepreneurship. The financial strength creates a sense of security against fear of failure. In the present study, it was intended to enquire into the financial strength of the past generation. While financial strength of the past generation stimulated the desire for entrepreneurship, the financial soundness of the present generation encourages the speed of the entrepreneurship.

The magnitude of entrepreneurs' activity also depends on the father's economic status. A study of this reveals the economic background inherited by the entrepreneurs. Some of them may

Table 10
Caste and Gender of the Entrepreneurs

Gender	*Caste of the Entrepreneurs*									
	Forward Caste		*Backward Caste*		*Schedule Caste*		*Schedule Tribe*		*Total*	
	No	%	*No*	%	*No*	%	*No*	%	*No*	%
Male	73(51)	84.9	50(35)	64.1	18(12.5)	66.66	2(1.4)	50	143(100)	72.95
Female	14(26.4)	16.1	28(53)	35.9	9(17)	33.34	2(3.6)	50	53(100)	27.05
Total	87	100	78	100	27	100	4	100	196	100

Note: Figures in parentheses represent percentages

The calculated value of chi-square =9.51

Table value of chi-square at 0.05 percent level=11.10

Source: Field Survey

show initiative in consolidating and building up on the base provided by their fathers and some may start from scratch and thus become self made entrepreneurs.

Table 11a
Income of the Entrepreneurs Father

Father's Income	*No of Entrepreneurs*	*Percentage*
More than Rs. 10,000/-	27	13.8
More than Rs. 25,000/-	59	30.1
More than Rs. 50,000/-	81	41.3
More than Rs. 75,000/-	22	11.2
More than Rs. 1,00,000/-	7	3.6
Total	196	100.0

Median = 43.70 Mode = 47.98.
Source: Field Survey

As shown in Table 11a that 41.3 percent of entrepreneurs father's income was more than Rs. 50,000/- per annum, 30.1 percent of entrepreneurs father's income were above Rs. 25,000/- and only 3.6 percent earning more than Rs. 1,00,000/- per annum. The median value of initial investment was 43.70.

Table 11b
Annual Income of the Respondent

Income	*No of Entrepreneurs*	*Percentage*
Up to 1 lakh	42	21.4
Rs. 1,00,001 to Rs. 5,00,000	91	46.4
Rs. 5,00,001 to Rs. 10,00,000	53	27.0
Rs. 10,00,001 to Rs. 15,00,000	10	5.1
Above Rs.15,00,000	-	-
Total	196	100.0

Median = 40.81 Mode = 30.82
Source: Field Survey

The Economic background of the entrepreneurs is viewed on the basis of annual earnings of the entrepreneur from various sources. The Table 11b that the annual earnings of 46.4 percent of the entrepreneurs (91 out of 196) were between Rs. 1,00,001–Rs. 5,00,000, 21.4 percent earned less than Rs. 1,00,000, 27 percent were earning between Rs. 5,00,001–Rs. 10,00,000. Only 5.1 percent were earning Rs. 15, 00,000 and above. The median annual income is 40.81.

The above trend demonstrates that economic status has been increasing from generation to generation. This elevation leads to increased entrepreneurial activity breeding new class of entrepreneurs.

Annual Income and Form of Ownership

The Table 12 given below shows the relational distribution of the respondents on the basis of their annual income and form of organization.

It could be seen in the Table 12 that 64.28 percent of respondents of proprietary concern were earning only Rs. 1 lakh where as earnings of the partnership firms were more than the earnings of the proprietary concerns.

The chi-square value clearly shows that these two variables are not having significant association. The calculated value of chi-square with two degrees of freedom(3.43) is found to be very less than the theoretical value at 0.05 percent level(7.38) and it may be concluded, therefore, that both proprietary and partnership earnings are good.

Annual Income and Age of Entrepreneur

The Table 13 shows distribution of respondents' annual income and age of the entrepreneurs.

The information presented in the Table 13 clearly shows that about 52.2 percent of the respondents earning annual income Rs. 1,00,001 to 5, 00,000 were between 26-35 years of age. Further, 37.5 percent of the respondents' age was between 36-50 years and were earning Rs. 500,001 to Rs. 10, 00,000 per annum.

Table 12
Annual Income and Form of Ownership

	Income of Entrepreneurs									
	Upto 1 lakh		*Rs. 1,00,001 to Rs. 5,00,000*		*Rs.5,00,001 to Rs. 10 lakhs*		*Rs. 10,00,001 to Rs. 15,00,000*		*Total*	
Form of Ownership	*No*	*%*	*No*	*%*	*No*	*%*	*No*	*%*	*No*	*%*
Proprietary	27(25.4)	64.28	50(47.2)	54.94	25(23.5).	47.16	4(3.8)	40	106(100)	54.08
Partnership	9(11.8)	21.42	34(44.8)	37.36	27(35.6)	50.96	6(7.8)	60	76(100)	38.77
Private Ltd	2(25)	4.76	5(62.5)	5.50	1(12.5)	1.88	-	-	8(100)	4.08
Public Ltd	4(80)	9.54	1(20)	1.10	-	-	-	-	5(100)	2.55
Others	-	-	1(100)	1.10	-	-	-	-	1	0.52
Total	42	100	91	100	53	100	10	100	196	100

Note: Figures in parentheses represent percentages
The calculated value of chi-square =3.43
Table value of chi-square at 0.05 percent level=7.38

Source: Field Survey

Table 13

Annual Income and Age of the Entrepreneur

Age of Entrepreneur	*Income of Entrepreneurs*									
	Upto 1 lakh		*Rs. 1,00,001 to Rs. 5,00,000*		*Rs.5,00,001 to Rs. 10 lakhs*		*Rs. 10,00,001 to Rs. 15,00,000*		*Total*	
	No	*%*	*No*	*%*	*No*	*%*	*No*	*%*	*No*	*%*
Below &25 yrs	10(35.7)	23.80	13(46.4)	14.28	5(17.9)	9.43	-	-	28(100)	14.28
26-35 yrs	21(23.9)	50	46(52.2)	50.54	20(22.7)	37.73	1(1.2)	10	88(100)	44.89
36-50 yrs	10(13.8)	23.80	27(37.5)	29.69	27(37.5)	50.94	8(11.2)	80	72(100)	36.73
Above 50 yrs	1(12.5)	2.4	5(62.5)	5.49	1(12.5)	1.81	1(12.5)	10	8(100)	4.10
Total	42	100	91	100	53	100	10	100	196	100

Note: Figures in parentheses represent percentages

The calculated value of chi-square =7.21

Table value of chi-square at 0.01 percent level=7.38

Source: Field Survey

The value of chi-square shows that there is no significant association between income and age of entrepreneur. The calculated value of chi-square(7.21) is found to be less than the theoretical value(7.38) at 0.01 percent level with two degrees of freedom. It may be concluded that the respondents in the age group of 26-50 years were earning more.

Annual Income and Gender of the Entrepreneur

The Table 14 given below shows the distribution of the respondents on the basis of their annual income and gender.

It could be observed from the Table 14 that 46.2 percent of respondents' earnings between Rs. 1,00,001 to Rs. 5,00,000 were males, similarly 47 percent of female respondents were also earnings between Rs. 1,00,001 to Rs. 5,00,000 per annum.

The chi-square test, revealed a computed value of (0.15) which is very less than the theoretical value (11.10) at 0.05 percent level with four degrees of freedom. It indicates that there was no significant association between male and female income. It leads to conclusion that female entrepreneurs were earnings equally along with male entrepreneurs.

Annual Income and Educational Qualification of the Entrepreneurs

The following Table 15 shows the distribution of respondents on the basis of annual income and their educational qualification of entrepreneurs.

The Table 15 reveals that 66.6 percent of uneducated were earning upto 1 lakh where as 54 percent of SSC holders were earning between Rs. 1,00,001 to Rs. 5,00,000 and 51 percent of graduates were also earning the same.

The value of the chi-square indicates a significant association between these variables. The computed value of chi-square (21.31) which is higher than the theoretical value (10.60) at 0.01 percent level with two degrees of freedom. It refers to the conclusion that educated entrepreneurs' earnings were good. Thus formal

Table 14
Annual Income and Gender of Entrepreneur

Gender	Income of Entrepreneurs									
	Upto 1 lakh		*Rs. 1,00,001 to Rs.5,00,001*		*Rs. 5,00,000 to Rs. 10 lakhs*		*Rs. 10,00,001 to Rs. 15,00,000*		*Total*	
	No	%	No	%	No	%	No	%	No	%
Male	30(21)	71.42	66(46.2)	72.52	39(27.2)	73.58	8(5.6)	80	143(100)	72.95
Female	12(22.8)	28.58	25(47)	27.43	14(26.4)	26.42	2(3.8)	20	53(100)	27.05
Total	42	100	91	100	53	100	10	100	196	100

Note: Figures in parentheses represent percentages
The calculated value of chi-square =0.15
Table value of chi-square at 0.05 percent level=11.10

Source: Field Survey

Table 15

Annual Income of the Entrepreneurs and Educational Qualification

Education	Income of Entrepreneurs									
	Upto 1 lakh		Rs. 1,00,001 to Rs. 5,00,000		Rs.5,00,001 to Rs. 10 lakhs		Rs. 10,00,001 to Rs. 15,00,000		Total	
	No	%	No	%	No	%	No	%	No	%
Uneducated	4(66.6)	9.52	1(16.7)	1.10	1(16.7)	1.88	-	-	6(100)	3.06
School Dropout	9(41)	21.42	10(45.4)	10.10	3(13.6)	5.66	-	-	22(100)	11.22
SSC	16(32)	38.11	27(54)	29.67	5(10)	9.45	2(4)	20	50(100)	25.52
Graduate	12(12.2)	28.57	50(51)	54.94	35(35.8)	66.03	1(1)	10	98(100)	50.0
PG & above	1(5)	2.38	3(15)	3.29	9(45)	16.98	7(35)	70	20	10.20
Total	42	100	91	100	53	100	10	100	196	100

Note: Figures in parentheses represent percentages
The calculated value of chi-square =21.31
Table value of chi-square at 0.01 percent level=10.60

Source: Field Survey

education is always considered an important asset to an entrepreneur.

Annual Income and Caste of the Entrepreneurs

The following Table 16 shows the caste wise distribution of respondents on the annual income.

As shown in Table 16, 54 percent of the forward caste were earning between Rs. 1,00,001 and Rs. 5,00,000, similarly 42.6 percent of backward caste earnings were also between Rs. 1,00,001 to Rs. 5,00,000. 44.4 percent of scheduled caste were earning up to 1 lakh.

It leads to the conclusion that inspite of government concessions and reservation, lesser number of scheduled castes are venturing into the entrepreneurship. The values of chi-square indicate a moderately significant association between these variables. The calculated value of chi-square (11.52) at four degrees of freedom is higher than the theoretical value (11.10) at 0.05 percent level strengthens the above statement.

MOTIVATIONAL FACTORS

Having studied the socio-economic background of entrepreneurs in the previous section, it is intended to study the entrepreneurial motivation. Analysis of the factors that have motivated and facilitated the emergence of entrepreneurship in the Nellore district is the goal of this section.

ENTREPRENEURSHIP MOTIVATION

The statement that people are poor because their preference was one of the causes of poverty attributed by Galbraith for the backwardness of many Asian and African nations. Galbraith further elucidated that because the people of these nations are lacking in motivation, they are lagging behind others in development[19].

The biggest obstacle to progress in India is also deemed to be the "limited aspirations" of her people[20]. Motivation motivates

Table 16
Annual Income and Caste of the Entrepreneurs

Caste	*Income of Entrepreneurs*									
	Upto 1 lakh		*Rs. 1,00,001 to Rs. 5,00,000*		*Rs.5,00,001 to Rs. 10 lakhs*		*Rs. 10,00,001 to Rs. 15,00,000*		*Total*	
	No	*%*	*No*	*%*	*No*	*%*	*No*	*%*	*No*	*%*
Forward Caste	13(15)	30.96	47(54)	51.64	22(25.2)	41.50	5(5.8)	50	87(100)	44.38
Backward Caste	16(20)	38.09	33(42.6)	36.28	25(32)	47.16	4(5.4)	40	78(100)	39.79
Schedule Caste	12(44.4)	28.57	9(33.3)	9.89	5(18.5)	9.46	1(3.8)	10	27(100)	13.77
Schedule Tribe	1(25)	2.38	2(50)	2.19	1(25)	1.88	-	-	4(100)	2.06
Total	42	100	91	100	53	100	10	100	196	100

Note: Figures in parentheses represent percentages
The calculated value of chi-square =11.52
Table value of chi-square at 0.05 percent level=11.10

Source: Field Survey

men, activates them, broadens their vision and makes the life meaningful. Motivation is an index of one's own resourcefulness. Like an individual, nations or regions or families may have their own motives which speak of their resourcefulness.

The motives builds up achievement "pressure" in the individual concerned and it seems reasonable to infer that he has a strong "inner urge" with achievement. This "pressure" or "inner concern" provides the basis for McClelland's n-factor (the need for achievement factor) ratings[21]. Assuming "need for achievement" plays a vital role in promoting economic growth. McClelland wondered whether it would not be possible to induce achievement motivation in adults and provide them with an urge to improve their lot since uninduced achievement motivation results in long waiting before it bears fruit. Such an inducement may help break the barrier of "limited aspirations". In this direction a full fledged programme was undertaken by McClelland at Kakinada in Andhra Pradesh. Earlier preliminary studies were undertaken with groups of businessmen in Mexico City, Mumbai and the United States of America.

Kakinada was well developed district town with a high literacy and modest industrial infrastructure having population around one lakh. The objective of the programme was to break the barrier of "limited aspirations" by inducing achievement motivation. The project which began in January, 1964 consisted of recruiting batches of personnel, drawn from business and industrial community of the town and putting them through orientation programmes at the "Small Industry Extension Training Institute (SIET), Hyderabad. In all 52 persons participated in this programme. The training there was designed primarily to stimulate the imagination and encourage introspection into personal motivation and community goals. McClelland concluded that those who were exposed to the programme, displayed a more active business behaviour (51 percent as against 25 percent in the control group) and worked for longer hours. Significantly, he found that caste, traditional beliefs or western ways of life did not determine the mental make up of a participant but the training given at Hyderabad was likely to improve those who have great yearning to do something and have the opportunity to do so in their business framework [22].

The Kakinada experiment was being utilized in a number of experiments that were recently initiated for technical personnel to set up new enterprises of their own. The Gujarat programme has been successful in persuading many persons to set up new enterprises in the small scale sector. Similarly, the Andhra Pradesh Small Scale Industrial Development Corporations Ltd., (APSSIDC) has been assisting orientation programme at the SIET institutue[23].

It has been realized that entrepreneurship is to be developed from an early age. In this connection, the Ford Foundation conducted a pilot project study under the direction of Eugena Staley. Staley selected one district in Maharashtra (Osmanabad) for the pilot study and developed a school curriculum that would provide a high degree of motivation among the students. He introduced the success stories drawn from history and legends of the indigenous cultures to induce in young minds the sense of "need for achievement" and the desire to do something after they grow up[24].

Interest in similar programme was evinced in the USA and UK. In the United States, a junior achievement programme has been working for many years as an educational activity through which 40,000 boys and girls are engaged in making and selling products as an after school activity. They are helped by 14,000 corporations whose employees act as guides and philosophers of the miniature enterprises. Each company begins its operation when the school opens and dissolves itself after nine months when the vacation begins[25].

Ambition is the lever of all motives. The intentions and initiatives of a man are directed by his ambitions. It is the ambition that electrifies man's actions. The common saying "aimless life is a goalless game" emphasizes the importance of ambition in life.

So, what matters much is not merely the men but their motivations and means to reach their goal. It is the duty of the parents, the teachers and the leaders of the nation to instil motivation into the minds of the young people. Naturally, ambitions differ from individual to individual on the basis of personal tastes and temperaments, and family to family and nation to nation depending upon the circumstances in which they are placed and the priorities which they have set for themselves. Sometimes, personal motivation comes in the way of family ambitions or national ambitions. But the ambitions which are unfulfilled are passed on to the next generation who may chase the target with redoubled efforts and vigour. So ambitions which nourish the achievement motivation, brings in economic growth and development. Ambition is not something which is akin to greed or windfall. Greed results in disaster and windfall makes one a speculator [26]. This study proposes to enquire into factors of entrepreneurial motivations.

Motives for Starting an Enterprise

This study proposes to enquire into entrepreneurial motives and facilitating factors and motivators in the cast of entrepreneurs. It could be seen from the Table 16 motives for starting an enterprise.

Table 16
Motivating Factor

Motivating factor	*Number*	*Percentage*
Self employment.	59	30.1
Continue the same family business.	53	27.0
Dissatisfaction with the present Job.	45	23.0
Eagerness to make money.	31	15.8
Gain social prestige	6	3.1
Others.	2	1.0
Total	196	100

Source: Field Survey

The Table 16 shows that 30.1 percent of the entrepreneurs have started the enterprise to be self employed, 27 percent wanted to continue the family business where as 23 percent were dissatisfied with the present job. However, 15.8 percent of entrepreneurs started their enterprise to make money. The social prestige is insignificant.

It could be inferred that self employment, dissatisfaction with present job, continuing the family business and to make money was key drivers for entering into entrepreneurial activity.

Persons Influenced to Start the Enterprise

Having identified the motivating factors, an effort is made to find out the persons who have influenced the entrepreneurs to start their own business are presented in the below Table.

Table 17
Person Influenced to Start the Enterprise

Person	*Number*	*Percentage*
Self	12	6.1
Spouse	30	15.3
Family Members	115	58.7
Friends	30	15.3
Relatives and Others	9	4.6
Total	196	100.0

Source: Field Survey

It was observed that 58.7 percent of the promoters were influenced by their family members, 15.3 percent each were influenced by friends and spouse, 6.1 percent were influenced by themselves, and rest by relatives. It is evident that as many as (74%) of entrepreneurs had direct support from their family members and spouse to start their new ventures, which is a healthy signal for economic development of the country.

Initial Source of Finance to Start the Business

The initial sources of finance to start the business are presented in the Figure below.

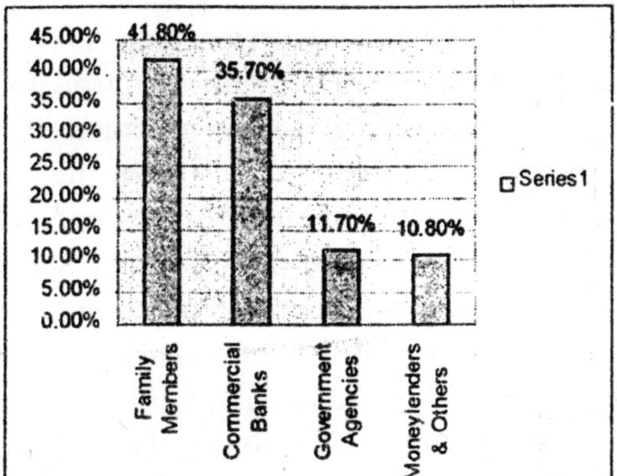

Source: Field Survey

Figure 4: Initial Source of Finance

The Figure 4 shows that 41.8 percent of the entrepreneurs had raised the finance support from family members, 35.7 percent from commercial banks, 11.7 percent from government agencies and remaining 10.8 percent from money lenders.

The financial help from the family members of the entrepreneur is to be considered as an important and strategic one. Firstly, it indicates the confidence of the family in the capabilities of the entrepreneur and profitability of the activity. Secondly, it indicates the preparedness of the family to risk its savings in an entrepreneurial activity. On the top of these, it is a torch bearer in shaping the entrepreneur's new career. From this, it is acknowledged that family members are encouraging the entrepreneurship development.

Training Programme

Entrepreneurial Development Models(ED)[27] have been formulated in order to identify and select the prospective entrepreneurs so as to give training to these first generation entrepreneurs to carry out the various industrial activities successfully. ED–models have been designed to promote the entrepreneurial development at several stages The ED–model that has been formulated by the Entrepreneurship Development Institute of India (ED–model–EDII) aims at providing the right type of entrepreneurial training and the provision of follow–up–support for the entrepreneurs to sustain the industrial activities. ED-model of EDII indicates that the careful selection of the entrepreneurs has to be done in order to identify the potential entrepreneurs by assessing the technical and managerial capabilities, and potentialities of the entrepreneurs and the risk–taking capabilities, aptitude and the social background. To augment the supply of entrepreneurs for promoting the entrepreneurial qualities, this ED–model intends to provide training for the entrepreneurs to acquire capabilities by promoting the awareness in the entrepreneurs. The model has been formulated to offer training in the aspects connected with project planning and in decision-making regarding product choice, market expansion, the utilization of subsidies and other incentives offered by the government and in the maintenance of cordial relations with employees/workers and in managing the industrial unit successfully.

The ED–model contemplates the offering of post–training for the entrepreneurs in the various aspects by considering the success and achievement in order to strengthen and sustain the industrial activities by the entrepreneurs. This model further intends to provide the entrepreneurial counselling and opportunity guidance and management appreciation programme to facilitate the industrial development.

Entrepreneurial Development programme model of Small Industries Extension and Training (ED-model–SIET) intends to promote the prospective and successful entrepreneurs and try to fill the gap between the supply of entrepreneurs and demand for these entrepreneurs. This ED-model is an integrated Model formulated for the promotion of entrepreneurs covering the aspects that are grouped as stimulatory, supportive and sustained. In this ED–model of SIET, the entrepreneurs education has been assigned priority in the stimulatory stage to increase the entrepreneurs' opportunities through the identification of potential entrepreneurs in a given area, and motivating them by providing the economic insights, and assist these entrepreneurs in selecting new industrial activities/areas by preparing the project feasibility reports for these industrial activities. This model aims at the setting up of the local entrepreneurial promotional agencies with the necessary executives and personnel for providing the entrepreneurial motivation and counseling and the creation of entrepreneurial forms to discuss the achievement and success and the problems of the entrepreneurs, in order to recognize the promising and prospective entrepreneurs for increasing the supply of the entrepreneurs so as to facilitate the development of industrial activities.

The ED-model of SIET also envisages in training the entrepreneurs pertaining to the supportive activities related to the establishment of the industrial unit, particularly in the mobilization of finances and the availability of infrastructural facilities including buildings. This model aims at the extension of consultancy services for the entrepreneurs in the selection of technology and suitable plant and machinery and the possibilities of acquiring the raw materials and in the utilization of power, water and other common facilities and on the available tax reliefs and concessions and the marketing expansion possibilities, for improving the entrepreneurial activities so as to develop the quality of entrepreneurship. This ED- model further envisages to train the entrepreneurs in sustaining the activities related to the efficient management of the industry, in order to maintain the profitability so as to promote the entrepreneurial development by considering modernization and diversification of the industries of these entrepreneurs in order to improve the entrepreneurial supply while, ensuring the quality.

In such a background it was intended to examine whether entrepreneurs under study have attended any training programme before starting their enterprises.

Table 18
Entrepreneurs Attended Training Programme

Responses	*No. of Entrepreneurs*	*Percentage*
Yes	41	20.9
No	155	79.1
Total	196	100

Note: The calculated value of Z-test =11.52
Table value of Z-test at 0.01 percent level=2.58

Source: Field Survey

It is observed from the Table 18, out of the 196 entrepreneurs only 20 percent attended the training programmes before starting their enterprises. The calculated value of Z-test (11.52) is found to be higher than the Table value (2.58) at 0.01 percent level. This indicates that there is significant difference between these variables i.e., most of the entrepreneurs were not interested to attend the training programmes.

Table 18a
Entrepreneurs Reasons for not Attending Training Programmes

Reasons	*No. of entrepreneurs*	*Percentage*
Not Useful	35	22.5
Expensive	20	12.9
Inconvenient	30	19.3
Not aware of them	70	45.3
Total	155	100.0

Source: Field Survey

Table 18b
Entrepreneurs Source of Training

Programmes	*No. of Entrepreneurs*	*Percentage*
SFC	4	9.8
Commercial banks	8	19.6
EDPs	6	14.6
Family Business	23	56.0
Total	41	100.0

Source: Field Survey

Out of 155 entrepreneurs from Table 18a, 62 were not aware of such programmes, 22.5 percent of them felt of no use, 19.3 percent of expressed that it was not convenient to attend the training programmes, 12.9 percent of them felt, training programmes were expensive.

Among the 41 entrepreneurs from Table 18b who have undergone the training, 56 percent of them were trained by their family members, 19.6 percent by commercial banks and rest of them received training through entrepreneurship developing programmes organized by the District Industries Centre and State Financial Corporations

The above analysis indicates, inspite of intensified promotional activity by both state and central government, through their various agents like Entrepreneurship Development Institute of India, Ahmedabad, National Institute for Entrepreneurship and Small Business Development, New Delhi, Small Industries Development Bank of India, Lead Banks of each district, District Industries Centre, State Financial Corporations etc failed to create an awareness about the training programme among the budding entrepreneurs.

Reasons for not Attending Training Programmes and Form of Ownership

The relationship between the form of organization and reasons for not attending training programmes is being presented in the Table 19

From the Table 19, 62.9 percent of proprietors, 32.25 percent of partners were not aware of training programmes.

The value of chi-square shows that there is no significant association between these variables. The calculated value of chi-square (12.13) is found to be lesser than the theoretical value (12.80) at 0.01 percent level with three degrees of freedom. Therefore, the government agencies listed above should have relooked into the training programmes and made Entrepreneurial Development Programmes more useful friendly and meaningful.

Table 19
Reasons for not Attending Training Programmes and Form of Ownership

Form of Ownership	Reasons										Total	
	Not useful		*Expensive*		*Inconvenient*		*Not aware of them*		*Others*			
	No	*%*	*No*	*%*	*No*	*%*	*No*	*%*	*No*	*%*	*No*	*%*
Proprietary	11(12.6)	31.42	14(16.2)	70	17(19.6)	56.66	39(44.8)	62.90	6(6.8)	75	87(100)	56.12
Partnership	18(32.8)	51.42	6(10.9)	30	9(16.3)	30	20(36.3)	32.25	2(3.7)	25	55(100)	35.48
Private Ltd	2(25)	5.74	-	-	4(50)	13.34	2(25)	3.22	-	-	8(100)	5.16
Public Ltd	4(80)	11.42	-	-	-	*	1(20)	1.63	-	-	5(100)	3.24
Total	35	100	20	100	30	100	62	100	8	100	155	100

Note: Figures in parentheses represent percentages
The calculated value of chi-square =12.13
Table value of chi-square at 0.01 percent level=12.80

Source: Field Survey

Government Assistance

Government plays vital role in helping the enterprises by providing financial support and other infrastructural facilities. This Table 20 shows that 68.9 percent of the entrepreneurs availed government assistance. The value of Z-test shows that there is significant difference between the opinions of the entrepreneurs. The calculated value of Z-test (7.48) is found to be higher than the Table value (2.58) at 0.01 percent level strengthens the above statement.

Table 20a
Availing of Government Assistance

Response	*No of Entrepreneur*	*Percentage*
Yes	135	68.9
No	61	31.1
Total	196	100

Note: The calculated value of Z-test =7.48
Table value of Z-test at 0.01 percent level=2.58

Source: Field Survey

Having ascertained the extent of government assistance availed by entrepreneurs an attempt is made to find out different types of assistance availed by entrepreneurs from the government. The entrepreneurs have availed different types of assistance.

The results of the responses are presented in the Table below. The entrepreneurs seeking more than one assistance from government.

Table 20b
Type of Government Assistance

Type of Assistance	*No. of Units*	*Percentage*
Financial support	98	72.5
Promotional activities	60	44.4
Procurement of raw material	40	29.6
Site location	32	23.7

Multiple responses were allowed (*n=135)
Source: Field Survey

The Table 20b shows that 72.5 percent availed the financial support, 44.4 percent took the marketing assistance to promote their products, 29.6 percent of them approached government agencies for the procurement of raw material and 23.7 percent to locate the enterprise.

It is evident from the Table 20b that a majority (about 72.5 percent) of the respondents have availed financial support from the institutions.

Reasons for Starting an Enterprise in his/her Town

The place of activity influences the growth of entrepreneurship. The infrastructure offered by the place in terms of raw materials, labour, transport facilities, communication system and its proximity to the developing towns or cities attracts and stimulates the spirit of entrepreneurship. The entrepreneur's reasons for choosing town are shown in the Table 21.

Table 21
Entrepreneur's Reason for Starting an Enterprise in his/her Town

Reasons	*No of Entrepreneurs*	*Percentage*
Low Cost of Resources	74	37.8
Availability of Raw Material	72	36.7
Availability of Labour	17	8.7
Transport facilities	7	3.6
Others	26	13.3
Total	196	100.0

Source: Field Survey
* Others includes home town, nearness to market, availability of own plot in the home town etc.

The low cost and availability of raw material were important reasons for the selection of town. 37.8 percent selected the place because of the resources available at lesser cost, where as 36.7 percent were attracted by the availability of raw material, 13.3 percent of entrepreneurs have chosen the place because of the hometown, nearness to the market and availability of the plot.

8.7 percent of them were attracted by the availability of labour and 3.6 percent of them were impressed by transport facilities.

GROWTH FACTORS

Growth may be measured in terms of the increased employment, fixed assets, investment, production, profits, sales etc. In order to understand the growth of the entrepreneurship taken up by the respondents, several questions were included in the interview schedule pertaining to some basic characteristics of the enterprises being run by the entrepreneurs. The information obtained has been presented in this section.

Year of Establishment of Business

The Figure 5 shows the distribution of respondents on the basis of the year of establishment of their business. It is quite apparent from the distribution that a majority of the entrepreneurs (about 45.91 percent) have established their enterprise between 1990 and 1995. Out of 196 enterprises only 27 started their business before 1990, however their number by almost tripled (90) with in the span of five years (1990–1995). Later during 1995 -2000, another 79 enterprises (40.30 percent) were established. This is definitely a noticeable change in the district of Nellore, a sign of growth of entrepreneurship

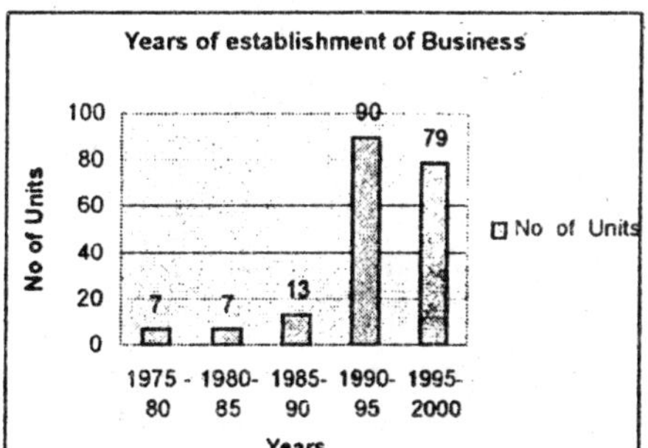

Figure 5

During the post–liberalization period, the small enterprises have grown phenomenally, indicating the conduciveness of the environment created by the government for the growth and development of entrepreneurship in Nellore district.

Investment in Enterprise

Availability of finance is an important prerequisite for establishing any entrepreneurial activity. Initially every entrepreneur should have finance of his/her own, out of the total cost of the project. Initial capital refers to venture or risk capital required for the establishment of a unit. The responses obtained are presented in the following Table.

Table 22

Comparison of Investment between the Initial and Latest Years

	No of Units		*Percentages*		
Investment (Rs in lakhs)	*Initial year*	*Latest year*	*Initial year*	*Latest year*	*Change (Percent)*
1-2	62	45	31.8	22.9	-27.98
3-4	45	32	22.9	16.4	-28.38
5-6	34	28	17.3	14.3	-17.34
7-8	22	30	11.2	15.4	37.5
9-10	20	34	10.2	17.3	69.6
11 & above	13	27	6.6	13.7	107.57
Total	196	196	100.0	100.0	

Source: Field Survey

From the above Table, it is evident that 31.8 percent of the units (62 out of 196) had an investment of less than 2 lakhs rupees. Another 22.9 percent of the units (45 out of 196) had an initial investment between Rs. 3 lakh and Rs. 2 lakhs. 17.3 percent of the units (34 out of 196) had an initial investment between Rs. 5 lakh and Rs. 6 lakhs. The rest of the units (55 out of 196) were started with an investment of Rs. 7 lakhs and above. Of them, only 13 units had an initial investment of Rs. 11 lakhs and above. The Table gives the frequency distribution of investment at the end of initial and latest years. Relative frequencies (percentages) and the percentages changes between initial and latest years are also shown alongside. It would be seen from the Table that number of units with an investment more than 7 lakhs as increased from 55 units to 91 units where as number of units with an investment less than 6 lakhs as decreased from 141 to 85 units.

It would be inferred from the above Table the units with less investment had graduated to large investment in the later year. It could be seen from the above Table that the enterprises under study have registered growth in their investment over the years.

Loan taken for Initial Investment

The Government of India and Reserve Bank of India have been instrumental in devising a multi-agency system for credit flow to small scale industries sector. The distinctive feature of the multi-agency set up is that the financial institutions have been extending term loans and banks are catering to the working capital requirements of the small scale enterprises. Of late, the distinction between the banks and financial institutions is gradually getting blurred and their roles are overlapping.

Table 23a
Information About Whether Loan Has Been Taken for Initial Investment

Response	*No of Entrepreneurs*	*Percentage*
Yes	151	77
No	45	23
Total	196	100

Note: The calculated value of Z-test =10.71
Table value of Z-test at 0.01 percent level=2.58

Source: Field Survey.

At the apex level, Small Industries Development Bank of India provides refinance to state level institutions such as State Financial Corporations (SFCs) and State Industrial Development

Corporations (SIDCs), besides extending direct assistance to the Small Scale enterprises. At the state level, State Financial Corporations provide assistance to small and medium industries in their respective areas of operation.

Availability of finance is an important prerequisite for establishing any entrepreneurial activity. Initially every entrepreneur has to avail some finance of his/her own or loan from outside for the establishment of a unit. The information in this regard is depicted in the following Table 23a.

It is evident from the Table 23a that 151 respondents (77%) have taken loans for initial investment. The calculated value of Z-test (10.71) is found to be higher than the Table value (2.58) at 0.01 percent level. This indicates that there is significant difference between these variables. It may be concluded that one third of entrepreneurs did not take any loan because of high rate of interest, delay in getting loan sanction, corruptions etc.

The next question in this regard is to ascertain the sources of loan. The responses have been presented in the Table 23b. Entrepreneurs usually raise loans from more than one source. The loan for plant and equipment, land and building is raised from financial institutions. Entrepreneurs approach the commercial banks for their working capital requirements. Entrepreneurs also raise quick loans from friends and relatives and money lenders. Since, getting the loan from financial institutions and commercial banks is time-consuming.

Table 23b
Initial Source of Loan

Initial Source of Finance	*No. of Units*	*Percentage*
Financial Institutions	120	80
Relatives /Friends	90	59
Commercial Banks	80	53
Money lenders	60	40

Multiple responses were allowed (*n=151)
Source: Field Survey

The above Table shows that a very large proportion (about 80 percent) of the respondents have taken initially from financial institutions. On the other hand, 40 percent have acquired the loan from money lenders initially.

Thus, it is clear that, by and large, a substantial proportion of the respondents have taken initial source of loan from financial institutions and commercial banks.

Repayment of Loan

Having borrowed money from the financial institutions and commercial banks, entrepreneurs have to maintain its credit worthiness by repaying the loan with interest. If the entrepreneurs' credit worthiness is low, it becomes highly difficult to raise the loan. Hence, it was also important to examine the repayment of loan by the entrepreneurs, was asked in this regard. The paying practices are presented in the Table below.

Table 24
Repayment of Loan

Response	*No. of Entrepreneurs*	*Percentage*
Never defaulted	110	72.8
Some times defaulted	30	19.8
Usually defaulted	11	7.4
Total	151	100.0

* 45 respondents have not borrowed any loan. (Table 23a infra)
Source: Field Survey

A look at the above mentioned responses clearly shows that majority of (about 72.8 percent) the entrepreneurs have never defaulted in making repayment of the loan. About 19.8 percent of the respondents have occasionally defaulted in making repayment of their loan instalments. However only 7.4 percent have defaulted in making repayment.

The information leads to the conclusion that, the respondents repay their loan very regularly. The above information summarily explodes the myths relating to the non–credit–worthiness of small scale industry borrowers.

To be seen from Reserve Bank of India Report of India, the net bank credit flow to small scale sector has increased in absolute terms however its percent to total net bank credit is fluctuating from 15 to 16 percent during 1991 to 2000. It is clearly indicated that the largest of credit is going to the large scale industry.

Government Subsidies or Incentives

The Government of India and Government of Andhra Pradesh have been offering different types of incentives to small scale enterprises. The government has initially reserved 837 items for the small scale industries and these units produce over 7,500 commodities. The small enterprises were exempted from payment of EMD (Earning Monetary Deposit), Cost of Tender Schedules and 15% concessions in the rate purchase. It also offers backward area subsidies of 20% to the small enterprises located in backward area. Both the Centre and State Government offer a host of tax incentives like deferred tax payment, tax holidays etc. An attempt is made to analyze the awareness of entrepreneurs about subsidies and incentives provided by the government.

Table 25
Government Subsidies or Incentives

Responses	*No of Entrepreneur*	*Percentage*
Yes	102	52
No	94	48
Total	196	100

Note: The calculated value of Z-test =0.81
Table value of Z-test at 0.05 percent level=1.96

Source: Field Survey

The government has granted various subsidies or incentives for fostering small scale entrepreneurship in the state. Attempt is made to analyze as to how many entrepreneurs were attracted to start their enterprises because of subsidies or incentives. The Table 25 sets out information concerning grant of subsidies or incentives.

Of the total 196 entrepreneurs, 102 entrepreneurs (52 percent) are aware of subsidies or incentives available for their industry. Further, it may be concluded that the 94 entrepreneurs (48 percent) are not aware of the government subsidies and incentives, concessions and other facilities made available to their industry. The calculated value of Z-test (0.81) is found to be much lesser than the Table value (1.96) at 0.05 percent level. It indicates that there is no significant difference between proportions of opinions.

The government has to create awareness among the prospective entrepreneurs about various incentives and schemes that are offered to the small scale industries sector. Since about half of the entrepreneurs were not aware of the various schemes and incentives even after 57 years of independence.

Employment

Frequency distribution of employment in the initial and the latest year is shown in the Table 26.

Table 26
Comparison of Distribution of Employment Between the Initial and Latest Years

No of Employees	*No of Units*		*Percentages*		*Change (Percent)*
	Initial year	*Latest year*	*Initial year*	*Latest year*	
Below 10	114	94	58.2	47.9	-17.69
11-20	72	76	36.7	38.7	5.44
21 & above	10	26	5.1	13.4	162.74
Total	196	196	100.0	100.0	

Source: Field Survey

The Table 26 shows that more than one-half (58.26 percent) of the units employed less than 10 persons as at the end of initial year. Only 5.1 percent of the units (10 out of 196) employed more than 20. There is an marginal increase in the number of employees from the initial year to the latest year. The percentage of units employing more than 20 increased from 5.1 percent to 13.4 percent where as the percentage of units employing less than 10 decreased from 58.2 percent to 47.9 percent. The increase in the number of employees may be taken as an indicator of growth. The growth in the employment between the initial and the latest years suggests that the small scale units have grown fairly by providing more employment.

Training to Employees

The entrepreneurs were asked whether they provided any general training to their employees. The information obtained is depicted in the Table below.

Table 27
Information About Providing of Training to Employees

Provided	*No. of Entrepreneurs*	*Percentage*
Yes	63	32.1
No	133	67.9
Total	196	100.0

Note: The calculated value of Z-test =7.07
Table value of Z-test at 0.0 percent level=2.58

Source: Field Survey

67.9 percent have not provided any training to their employees. Remaining 32.1 percent provided training to their employees. The Z-test, revealed a computed value of (7.07) which is higher than the Table value (2.58) at 0.01 percent level. It indicates that there is a significant difference between proportions of opinion on providing of training to employees. It leads to the conclusion, that the entrepreneurs of small scale enterprises were not able to give importance to training programmes. The employees after receiving training migrate to the medium and large industries in search of new opportunities to grow.

Profits

In the economic theory, the behaviour of a firm is analyzed in terms of profit. The underlying logic is of profit efficiency. Profit is considered as the most appropriate resource of a firm's performance. The precise meaning of the profit is nuclear. Does it mean short-term or long-term profit? Does it refer to profit before tax or after tax? Since most of the entrepreneurs do not maintain their books of accounts. The accounts are maintained by their auditors. The entrepreneurs were reluctant to the part with the information about the qualitative of profit. The question related to profit is only qualitative to find out the number of years taken to make profit.

Table 28
Time Taken to Earn Profits

Period	*No of Units*	*Percentage*
With in one Year	92	46.9
With in two Year	77	39.3
With in three Year	20	10.2
With in four Year	5	2.6
With in five Year	2	1.0
Total	196	100.0

Source: Field Survey

Profit is one of the conditioning factors for assessing the performance of the small enterprise. Every enterprise irrespective of its size, has to earn a reasonable profit, to service its borrowings and a return for own investment. It could be seen from the Table 5.1.1 (infra) that majority of enterprises surveyed were proprietary and partnership concerns. Profit is required for reinvestment for the growth of expansion of business. The small units have many advantages because of their size. In other words, because of their scale of operation, their gestation period may be low and break even earlier which in turn helps in facilitating an early return on investments i.e., profits. As a matter of fact, it is important to mention here that a longer gestation period for a small unit may be disadvantages such as escalation of price of plant and machinery, burden of interest on loan capital, declining sales due to late entry of the product and so on and so forth.

From the Table 28, it was found that 92 units (46.9 percent) started earning profit with in the first year, 77 units (39.3 percent) during second year and 30 units (10.2 percent) during the third year. 5 units (2.6 percent) made profit during the fourth year and two during the fifth year. Probing into the reasons for a longer gestation period revealed the following.

The factors for delay are the

1. Procedural delay in sanctioning loan, faulty project report, delay in providing electricity connection and quota for raw materials etc.,
2. Some entrepreneurs lost enthusiasm during the period of promotion due to changed circumstances and hurdles which appeared during the process. They further opined that what was being propagated by the promotional organizations for the encouragement of potential entrepreneurs to start industry was not carried on by them further in a spirited manner.

Despite several hurdles in the process of establishing a unit, quite a large number of units (46.9 percent), however started earning profits during the first year of commencement. Very few cases in our study took more than 4 years to start to earn profits.

Growth in Profits

Ascertainment of profits in informal sectors is an uphill task for obvious reasons. The problems are more in the Indian context where the incidence of taxes is very much on the high side compared to the other countries. Concealment of the incomes and evasion of taxes are rampant in India. Incomes are concealed for non tax reasons also. Educational opportunities are offered free of cost or at concessional rate to the wards of those with meagre incomes, generally people making a living in the informal sector deliberately supress their incomes to take advantage of such free ships or concessions. More than any thing else, Indians in general have lot of aversion to reveal their profit figures. This aversion is caused by fear and suspicion in their mind.

The question related to the absolute figures of the profit is avoided since entrepreneurs are not at all interested in revealing the quantum of profit. The accounts are mostly maintained by their auditors. In the light of the above, the qualitative questions were proposed to ascertain the information about profitability of the enterprises. The trend in profits from enterprise is depicted in the Table below.

Table 29
Trend in Profits

Trend	*No. of Entrepreneurs*	*Percentage*
No Change	149	76.0
Decrease	30	16.3
Increase	17	8.7
Total	196	100.0

Source: Field Survey

It is evident from the Table that 76 percent reported that there is no change in profits during the last three years. Further, about 16.3 percent reported decline in profits and only 8.7 percent registered an increase in profits. This information leads to the conclusion that by and large, three fourth of the entrepreneurs are running their enterprises with constant profits.

Reinvestment of Profits

Having ascertained the growth in the profits, an attempt is made to find out the percentage of entrepreneurs who reinvested their profits for the growth and expansion of their enterprise.

It is evident from the Table30 that only about 49 percent of the entrepreneurs have reinvested their profits in the firm and remaining 51 percent did not reinvest their profits in the firm. The computed value of Z-test (0.40) is lesser than the Table value (1.96) at 0.05 percent level which supports the statement.

Table 30
Reinvestment of Profits in the Enterprise

Reinvestment	*No. of Entrepreneurs*	*Percentage*
Yes	96	49.0
No	100	51.0
Total	196	100.0

Note: The calculated value of Z-test =0.40
Table value of Z-test at 0.05 percent level=1.96

Source: Field Survey

The respondents were also asked about the reasons for not reinvesting their profits in the firm. It was an open ended question and the respondents were in the process of diversifying into another business, investing in share market and diverting the money into unproductive assets like house-construction.

Sales

The profitability of the firm depends upon its sales. Since, sales is an important growth indicator of an enterprise. Growth in the sales is an appropriate indicator of performance. It is considered very interesting and important to know about sales of the enterprise. Sales is a key function in any enterprise as it is responsible for making marketing decisions, like sales budgeting,

Table 31
Trend in Sales

Trend	*No. of Entrepreneurs*	*Percentage*
No change	151	77.0
Decrease	28	14.3
Increase	17	8.7
Total	196	100.0

Source: Field Survey

quotas and territories. The Table 31 shows the information in this regard.

It is very clear from the data that about 77 percent of the entrepreneurs reported constant sales during the last three years. 14.3 percent of entrepreneurs experienced decrease in sales and only 8.7 percent reported an increase in sales.

It would be inferred from the above Table 31, the small enterprises have remained stagnant by and large since insignificant number of enterprises registered increase in profits and sales.

Advertising

The practice of advertising dates back to ancient times when town criers walked the streets of ancient Athens announcing upcoming sales of goods, thus serving as the forerunners of radio advertisements. Advertising plays a very important role today. It is a powerful promotional tool used by businesses and non-business organizations for informing, persuading and reminding their targeted audiences. Advertising in the printed electronic media is quite expensive. Small scale enterprises cannot afford to advertise their product in the electronic media. Their responses have been illustrated in the Table below.

Table 32

Entrepreneur's Response Regarding Advertising of Products

Response	*No. of Entrepreneurs*	*Percentage*
Yes	72	36.7
No	124	63.3
Total	196	100.0

Note: The calculated value of Z-test =5.251
Table value of Z-test at 0.01 percent level=2.58

Source: Field Survey

The Table shows that 63.3 percent of the entrepreneurs did not advertise their products. Only 36.7 percent of entrepreneurs advertised their products. The calculated value of Z-test (5.251) is found to be higher than the table value (2.58) at 0.01 percent level. It indicates that there is significant difference between proportions of opinion on advertising of products.

Thus, it is seen that entrepreneurs, by and large, inspite of stagnant sales, did not go for advertising. This may be because of higher promotional cost of the advertising in electronic and print media.

Media of Advertising

Such of those respondents who advertised their products were asked to elaborate in the media chosen for advertising. The responses have been presented in the Table 33.

Table 33
Media of Advertising

Type	*No. of Entrepreneurs*	*Percentage*
Newspapers	38	52.77
Pamphlets	21	29.16
Television	13	18.07
Radio	–	–
Total	72	100.0

Source: Field Survey

A perusal of the data indicates that, 52.77 percent of the entrepreneurs have advertised in newspapers, 29.16 percent of the respondents used pamphlets and remaining 18.07 percent in television through the local cable network.

It is clear that majority of the entrepreneurs have advertised their products in less costly local cable network.

IMPACT OF GLOBALIZATION AND LIBERALIZATION

Globalization is the process of integrating various economies of the world without creating any hindrances in the free flow of goods and services, technology, capital and even labour or human capital. The term 'Globalization' has, therefore, four parameters[28].

1. Reduction of trade barriers to permit free flow of goods and services among nation-states.
2. Creation of environment in which free flow of capital can take place among nation-states.
3. Creation of environment, permitting free flow of technology and
4. Last, but not the least, from the point of view of developing countries, creation of environment in which free movement of labour can take place in different countries of the world.

According to Stiglitz[29], globalization is the closer integration of the countries and people of the world which has been brought about by the enormous reduction of costs of transportation and communications, and the breaking down of artificial barriers to the flow of goods and services, capital, knowledge and (to a lesser extent) people across borders.

Jagdish Bhagwati[30] defines globalization in the following words: "economic globalization constitutes integration of national economies into the international economy through trade, direct foreign investment (by corporations and multinationals), short-term capital flows, international flows, of workers and humanity generally, and flows of technology".

In a nutshell, globalization is considered as the engine of growth, technical advancement, raising productivity, enlarging employment and bringing about poverty reduction along with modernization.

Even before the introduction of economic reforms in 1991[31] following the inevitable globalization, the small scale industries sector was somewhat over-protected. The hope that the infant would grow into an adult who could be freed to face competition has been completely belied. The small industry never had a strong desire to grow into medium and large scale industries because of the benefits of protection given to it. Many of the policies also discouraged the growth of small scale units into large ones and had a stunting effect on manufacturing, employment and output growth. With globalization, they are now more exposed to severe competition both from large scale sector- domestic and foreign– and from the Multi National Companies.

The poor growth rate in the small scale industries sector during the post–liberalization period can be attributed to various factors such as the new policies of the government in the direction of liberalization and globalization without ensuring the interests or priority of the sector. Left at the mercy of lending institutions and promotional agencies that feel proud and comfortable serving big units and multinationals, the small scale industries sector has withered into a state of deterioration in the quality of its output, industrial sickness and retrograde growth.

The emerging economic scenario in the changed liberalized and competitive economic environment necessitated structural and fundamental changes in the policy framework put in place for the development of small scale industries, causing a shift in focus from protection to promotion. In the post–reforms period, the government took a number of steps including partial de-reservation, change in investment limits, facilities for foreign participation, establishment of growth centers, export promotion, marketing assistance, incentives for quality improvements, etc. Important among these are given below.

- Better to focus the attention on the problems of the small scale industries sector, a new Ministry of Small Scale Industries and Agro and Rural Industries was created on 14th October 1999, and later on it announced an *'Agenda for the Millennium'* policy.
- A new Credit Insurance Scheme was announced in the Budget (1999-2000) for the small scale industries security to banks and improving the flow of investment credit to small scale industries units, particularly export oriented and tiny units.

- The working capital limit for small scale industries units is determined by the banks on the basis of 20 percent of their annual turnover. The turnover limit for this purpose has been enhanced from Rs. 4 crore to Rs. 5 crore
- A national programme for rural industrialization has been announced, with a mission to set up 100 rural clusters every year, to give a boost to rural industrialization.

To co-ordinate the latest developmental with regard to World Trade Organisation (WTO), a cell has been set up in the office of the Development Commissioner (Small Scale Industries) to disseminate information to small scale industries' associations regarding recent developments, prepare policies for the small scale industries in tune with the WTO agreements and organize WTO sensitization seminars, workshops, etc.

Steps are being taken to accelerate the programme of small scale industries branches to ensure that every district and small scale industries cluster within the district is served by at least one specialized small scale industries bank branch. Furthermore, to improve the quality of banking services, small scale industries branches are being asked to obtain ISO certification.

To further help small scale industries entrepreneurs, the National Equity Fund Scheme was introduced under which, equity support is provided for projects upto the limit of Rs. 15 lakh which is further raised to Rs. 25 lakh.

The single window scheme of Small Industries Development Bank of India is also being extended to all the districts. Thus, under the new policy, emphasis has been laid on development of small scale sector by providing different facilities instead of providing different types of protection.

Globalization and Liberalization

In order to examine whether the globalization and liberalization have any impact on products of enterprise, a question was asked in this regard and the responses obtained are presented in the Table 34.

Table 34
Impact of Globalization and Liberalization on Products

Response	*No. of Entrepreneurs*	*Percentage*
Yes	24	12.2
No	172	87.8
Total	196	100.0

Note: The calculated value of Z-test =14.95
Table value of Z-test at 0.01 percent level=2.58

Source: Field Survey

A perusal of the data indicated that a majority of the respondents (about 87.8 percent) have mentioned that globalization and liberalization did not affect the products of enterprise while 12.2 percent were affected by globalization and liberalization. The calculated value of Z-test (14.95) is found to be higher than the Table value (2.58) at 0.01 percent level. It indicates that there is a significant difference between these proportionate of opinions.

Thus it may be concluded that, the entrepreneurs have felt that globalization and liberalization did not have any effect on products.

Entrepreneurs Response regarding the Effect of Globalization and Liberalization on the following Aspects

Globalization and liberalization have brought many changes in economy of India. In this regard, entrepreneurs undeniably do have to experience stress and challenges at the work place and at outside as well. The entrepreneurs were asked to mention "the effect of globalization and liberalization on the following aspects". The responses obtained are depicted in the Table 35 below. The response were asked to present their preference in Likert five point scale ranging from very high to very low. The Table 35 is prepared on the basis of weighted average score to study the impact of globalization and liberalization.

Table 35

Effect of Globalization and Liberalization

Aspects	*Weighted Average Score*	*Rank*
Expenditure on promotion	4.47	1
Quality consciousness	4.19	2
Threat from Multi National Companies	4.06	3
Expenditure on production	4.03	4
Cost consciousness	4.02	5
Expenditure on distribution	3.88	6
Cost of Ready and Development	3.83	7
Competitive spirit	3.80	8
Considering diversification	3.73	9
Percentage of business opportunities	3.55	10
Social concern	3.54	11
Government support	3.50	12.5
Need for achievement	3.50	12.5
Total revenue	3.10	14

Source: Field Survey

It could be seen from the Table 35 the globalization and liberalization have increased the promotional expenditure (1st rank) followed by quality consciousness (2nd rank) and threat from Multi National Companies (3rd rank). It could be observed further there is wide spread increase in the cost of production (4th rank), cost consciousness (5th rank) increase in the distribution expenditure (6th rank) and increase Ready & Development.

MAJOR PROBLEMS ENCOUNTERED

The aforesaid analysis was centered round in gauzing the magnitude of the growth, we now look into major problems faced by the enterprises from time to time. The problems may differ from place to place and between one industry and the other. Even within the same industry, the problems may differ from enterprise to enterprise and also from entrepreneur to entrepreneur. These problems may be multi-dimensional relating to raw materials, marketing, power, labour, finance, technical and guidance etc., All these problems ultimately affect the overall performance of the enterprise. If the problems have their reflections on the performance, the performance gives an idea of the magnitude of the problems. The better the performance, the fewer may be the problems. In other words, the greater the problem, the greater the non-performance of units leading to lesser growth in terms of measures chosen.

Having analysed the subsequent growth of the firms of different entrepreneurs under study, it will be appropriate to review to main problems which the entrepreneurs face in their efforts to develop the enterprises they have established. Their achievements in this respect serve to complete the picture of growth presented in the first part of this chapter. The problems faced by different types of entrepreneurs were dealt with separately, because the problems of a manufacturer cannot be compared with the problems of a service provider. The problems of medical entrepreneurs (nursing houses) cannot be compared with those of a manufacturer. This is because of varied nature of their entrepreneurial activities. For example, the agricultural entrepreneurship is mostly influenced by the vagaries of the nature and the government's pricing policies. A merchant is concerned with the hostility of the government and the society. A manufacturer is worried with the marketing of the finished product. A medical practitioner is worried about winning the confidence of the patients. A tax consultant is interested in getting more number of clients by enabling them to get maximum benefit out of tax planning and management. A practising lawyer is more concerned about the winning chances of his client in the court of justice.

In the light of the limitations cited above, it may not be appropriate to elucidate the problems of such varied nature of different entrepreneurial activities, with a set of structured common questions. The problems of different types of entrepreneurs were evaluated by means of extended informal interviews with the chosen entrepreneurs.

Major Problems

Small scale industries are facing different types of problems. Six major problems were identified for the study i.e., raw materials, marketing, labour, finance, power and technical & managerial

Table 36
Major Problems Encountered by the Entrepreneurs

Major Problems	*Mean*
Raw Materials	
High prices	8.91
Scarcity	8.03
Low Quality	7.65
Transport	3.74
Marketing	
Competition from small industries	9.17
Slackness in demand	7.26
Price control	5.41
Competition from large industries	4.56
Labour	
Absenteeism	8.53
Turnover	7.45
High rates of wages/salaries	7.38
Indiscipline	5.43
Frequent work stoppages	4.15
Finance	
Shortage of fixed capital	8.44
Shortage of working capital	7.83
High rates of interest	7.82
Redtapism	5.03
Power	
Uncertainty	4.56
High cost	4.20
Scarcity	4.10
Technical and Managerial Assistance	
Ineffective consultancy service provide by government	7.38
Non availability of skilled workers	7.11
Non availability of proficient managers	6.15

Source: Field survey

assistance and the assessments was done on five point likert scale ranging from 5 for very important to 1 for not important. The results are given in the Table 36.

It was noted from the Table 36 that among raw materials, high prices (mean 8.91), was one of the major problems faced by the entrepreneurs, followed by competition from small industries (mean 9.17) of marketing, absenteeism (mean 8.53) of labour, shortage of fixed capital (mean 8.44) of finance, uncertainty (mean 4.56) of power and ineffective consultancy service provided by the government (mean 7.38) of technical and managerial assistances.

From the responses, it was observed that marketing and the raw materials were the major problems faced by the entrepreneurs.

Analysis of Variance

To further ascertain the likely inter-group variations among the major problems, ANOVA was done. The results were given in the Table 37.

Table 37
ANOVA for Major Problems Encountered by Entrepreneurs

Source of Variation	*Sum of Squares*	*Df*	*Mean Square*	*F-Value*
Between groups(problems)	18.96	5	3.79	1.32^{NS}
Error	48.77	17	2.87	
Total	67.73	22		

Source: Field Survey
Note: NS–Not Significant at 0.0 5% level

It was found by ANOVA that there was no significant difference between among the major problems of the entrepreneurs (F=1.32) at 0.05 percent level. It leads to the conclusion that there is no influence among the problems and the entrepreneurs are facing various problems depending on its growth in performance and actual operations of the enterprises.

Complaint to Government Agencies

The entrepreneurs were asked whether they made any complaint to the government agencies about their problems. The responses are presented in the following Table.

Table 38a

Response for Complaint to Government Agencies

Response	*No. of Entrepreneurs*	*Percentage*
Yes	19	9.7
No	177	90.3
Total	196	100.0

Note: The calculated value of Z-test =15.96
Table value of Z-test at 0.01 percent level=2.58

Source: Field Survey

From the above Table, the majority (about 90.3 percent) of the respondents did not make any complaint to government agencies. Only 9.7 percent of the respondents made a complaint. The calculated value of Z-test (15.96) is found to be higher than the Table value (2.58) at 0.01 percent level. It indicates that there is a significant difference between the responses of entrepreneurs.

Table 38b

Entrepreneurs Received Favourable Response

Response	*No. of Entrepreneurs*	*Percentage*
Yes	5	26.31
No	14	73.69
Total	19	100.0

Note: The calculated value of Z-test =2.92
Table value of Z-test at 0.01 percent level=2.58

Source: Field Survey

It could be seen from the Table 38b, out of 19 respondents who have complained for the grievances to the government, only 5 out of them received the response. The calculated value of Z-test (2.92) is found to be slightly higher than the Table value (2.58) at 0.01 percent level supports the above statement. It clearly shows apathy of the government agencies towards the problems faced by entrepreneurs.

ENTREPRENEUR'S OPINION ON SUCCESS

Entrepreneurial Success Factors

An important aspect of the study is to know, the opinion of entrepreneurs about the factors that contributed to their success. Entrepreneurial success depends on various factors. These factors were measured on a five point Likert scale (5=very important; 4=important, 3=average, 2=somewhat important, 1= Not important). The weighted average score of specific items are presented in the Table 39.

Table 39
Factors for Success

Factors	*Weighted Average Score*	*Rank*
Support from family members /friends	4.35	1
Assistance from Government	4.11	2
Property inherited	3.93	3
Belong to major community	3.80	4
Technical and professional knowledge	3.60	5

Source: Field Survey

The most important factor for the success of entrepreneurs was the moral support from family members and the friends (1st rank). The timely assistance from the government and property were the next important factor (2nd and 3rd ranks). Surprisingly technical and professional knowledge was the least important factor.

It could be inferred from the above analysis the entrepreneurs derived their spirit and motivation initially from family members and friends.

Expectations from Government

Entrepreneurs expect some benefits from government to their enterprises. The factors were measured using a five point Likert Scale (5=very important to 1=not important). The weighted average score in this regard is presented in the following Table.

Table 40

Expectations from Government

Benefits	*Weighted Average Score*	*Rank*
Help in export marketing of product	4.52	1
Control labour Unions	4.21	2
Treat all businessmen equally	3.85	3

Source: Field Survey

The results suggest that the entrepreneurs expect the government to help in exporting their products, controlling the labour organization and treating all the entrepreneurs equally without any bias and nepotism. The globalization has made the enterprises to explore the possibility of exporting the products. They expect the government to curb the trade union activities.

Aspirations about their Children

In Japan, aspiration for independence and accomplishment is developed through education at home and at school where children are brought up on such exhortations as "Boys; be ambitious", and "Be a head of a hen, rather than a lion of a cow"[32]. At home, the mother's influence is prominent. At school, some teachers change their pupils seats according to their examination results and pupils compete for the "seat of honour" with redoubled energy[33]. Those who are not fitted for competition in the academic field may try to distinguish themselves in sports, artistic activities etc., In either case, their education is competition minded and trained for success in a competitive environment. This philosophy is clearly reflected in the motives inspiring entrepreneurs. "I wanted to be master of my own business", the Japanese entrepreneurs often say "however small it might be".

Indian homes and schools are miles apart to their counterparts in Japan in developing such motives among their children. Merit is often found to be a causality in the Indian Schools and Colleges. Indian parents not only seek admission for their wards out of the way, they also seek passes/classes and even ranks in the examinations through unscrupulous and shameful methods. The prevalent capitation fees system, even in the medical and engineering colleges, bears a testimony to the character of Indian parents and administrators of education. It is unfortunate that some times even entrepreneurship is viewed by the Indian parents as something akin to wrong doing and making money, because of symphoning off millions and millions of rupees of the exchequer by the contractors, in collusion with ministers and bureaucrats.

In such a background, it was intended to examine whether entrepreneurs under study were interested in grooming their children as entrepreneurs of tomorrow.

Table 41a
Aspirations about their Children

Aspirations	*No. of Entrepreneurs*	*Percentage*
Yes	25	12.8
No	171	87.2
Total	196	100.0

Note: The calculated value of Z-test =14.75
Table value of Z-test at 0.01 percent level=2.58

Source: Field Survey

The entrepreneurs desire to make their children also entrepreneurs, is shown in the Table 41a. Surprisingly 87.2 percent of the parents did not like their children to become entrepreneurs. 12.8 percent were only interested in seeing their sons/daughters as entrepreneurs. The calculated value of Z-test (14.75) is found to be higher than the Table value (2.58) at 0.01 percent level. It indicates that there is significant difference between proportions of opinions of entrepreneurs.

Table 41b
Aspirations about the Line of Activity of their Children

Type of Business	*No. of Entrepreneurs*	*Percentage*
As he/she likes	14	56.0
New Business	9	36.0
Existing Business	2	8.0
Total	25	100.0

Source: Field Survey

The Table 41b indicates only 8 percent of entrepreneurs wanted their children to continue the existing business, 36 percent of them wanted their children to start a new line of business and 56 percent of the parents did not want to interfere.

Table 41c
Entrepreneurs Preferences their Children's Line of Activity

Preferences	*No. of Entrepreneurs*	*Percentage*
As he /she likes	61	35.68
Engineers	42	24.56
Employee	34	19.88
Doctors	23	13.45
Any others	11	6.43
Total	171	100.0

Source: Field Survey
Others includes: IT and Software related jobs.

From the Table 41c, it is evident that 35.68 percent of the entrepreneurs wanted their children to join a profession of their liking, 24.56 percent of them to become engineers, 19.88 percent to be in government jobs, 13.45 percent as doctors. This does not mean that all of them were going to disband their activities. Most of the enterprises in the Nellore district are of modest size. Enterprises of such sort cannot accommodate all the family members. Normally it is the wish of the parents with two or more children to handover the business to one of them and to settle other children in other occupations.

Entrepreneurs Satisfaction about their Present Line of Business

The entrepreneurs were asked to mention their satisfaction in their present line of business. The responses are given in the Table below.

Table 42
Entrepreneurs Satisfaction Level in the Present Line of Business

Satisfied	*No. of Entrepreneurs*	*Percentage*
Yes	84	42.8
No	112	57.2
Total	196	100.0

Note: The calculated value of Z-test =2.83
Table value of Z-test at 0.01 percent level=2.58

Source: Field Survey

It is quite evident from the data presented in the Table that most (over half of the respondents i.e., 57.2 percent) were not satisfied with the present line of business and only 42.8 percent were satisfied with present line of business. The calculated value of Z-test (2.83) is found to be higher than the Table value (2.58) at 0.01 percent level. It indicates that there is significant difference between these variables.

Thus, we may conclude that, by and large, little above half of the respondents was not satisfied with their achievements.

Factors for Failure

It is equally important to know, the factors that have contributed to the failure. These factors were measured in five point Likert scale (5=very important to 1= Not important). The weighted average score of responses obtained in this regard is presented in the Table below.

Table 43
Factors for Failure

Factors	*Weighted Average Score*	*Rank*
Lack of Planning	4.06	1
Having more than one business	3.95	2
Participation in politics	3.50	3
Quick Expansion of Business	3.04	4

Source: Field Survey

The data presented in the Table shows that lack of planning was the important factor followed by having interest in more than one business, participation in politics and expansion of business quickly contributed to the failure.

Thus, it may be concluded that, by and large, entrepreneurs perceived that lack of planning is the most important factor for failure of entrepreneurship.

Entrepreneurs Future Business Plans

The entrepreneurs were asked to mention their future business plans. The responses obtained are presented in the following Table. The factors were measured in five point Likert scale (5=very important to 1=not important).The weighted average score has been taken in this regard as follows.

Table 44
Entrepreneurs Future Business Plans

Future Plan	*Weighted Average score*	*Rank*
Setting up new business	4.15	1
Change of Product line	3.69	2
Expansion of plant	2.53	3

Source: Field Survey

The entrepreneurs are planning to go for new business, change of product line and expansion of existing plant.

Thus, most of the entrepreneurs were not happy with the present line of business and wanted to enter into new business line.

REFERENCES

1. Stauworth, M.J.K and Curran, J. (1973), "Management Motivation in the Smaller Business, "A Gower Press Special Study, Essex, p.28.

2. (a) Adam Smith, specifically included the acquired and useful abilities of all the inhabitants or the members of the society in his concept of capital. (An enquiry into the nature and causes the Wealth of Nations, Common Ed., Random House Inc., 1937, Book II, p.265-266).

   (b) Alfred Marshall emphasized the importance of education "as a national investment" and in his view the most valuable of all of capital is that invested in human beings, Principles of Economics, 8th ed., Mac Millian, 1930, p. 216.

   (c) Simon Kuznets has pointed out that measures of capital formation based on fixed capital are deficient because they omit expenditure for education, non–profit research, health, recreation etc, which "contributed to economic growth by increasing the efficiency of a complex productive system," (six lecturers on Economic Growth, The Free Press of Glencoe, New York, 1958, p.77).

3. Prederick Harbinson, and Charles A. Myer (1968), "Education, Manpower and Economic Growth," Oxford and 1BH Publishing Co, Calcutta, p.13.

4. Nayudamma, Y. (1978), "Convocation Address, First Annual Convocation on 7th May, Kakatiya University, Warangal, Andhra Pradesh, p.4

5. Government of India (1975), Report of the Committee on Development of Small and Medium Entrepreneurs, Ministry of Industrial Development, New Delhi, p.17.

6. Nafgiger, E. Wayne (1970), "Relationship between Education and Entrepreneurship in Nigeris," The Journal of Developing Areas, Vol.4, No. 3, April, p. 350-352.

7. Everett E. Hagen (1968), The Economics of Development, Home Wood III: Richard D. Irwin, p. 7-15.

8. Kindleberger (1961), "Economic Development," Mc Graw-Hill, New York, p.86.

9. Hery, M.J. (1965), "Contrasting Factors in the Modernization of China and Japan", Simon Kaznets et al.(Eds)., Economic Growth: Brazil, India, Japan, N.C. Duke University Press, Dusham.

10. Landes, D.S. (1949), "French Entrepreneurship and Industrial Growth in the Ninteenth Century", Journal of Economic History, May, p. 45-61.

11. Nafziger, E.Wayne (1970), African Capitalism, A Case Study in Nigerian Entrepreneurship, Hoover Institution, Standford, 1977, "The Effect of the Nigerian Extended Family on Entrepreneurial Activity" Economic Development and Cultural Change, 18, No.1, October, 1969, p.21-23. "The Relationship between Education and Entrepreneurship in Nigeria", The Journal of Developing areas, 4th April, p. 349-360.

12. Peter Kilby, Ed., (1971), Entrepreneurship and Economic Development, The Free Press, New York, p.1-50.

13. Yousif, A.Syigh (1962), "Entrepreneurs of Lebanon: The Role of Business Leader in Developing Economy, Harvard University Press, Cambridge.

14. John, J. Carroll (1965), "The Philippino Manufacturing Entrepreneur: Agent and Product of Changes," Corroll University Press, ITHACO.

15. Alec, P. Alexander (1964), Greek Industrialists, An Economic and Social Analysis, Centre of Planning and Economic Research, Athens.

16. Gustar, F. Papanek (1962), "The Development of Entrepreneurship", American Economic Review, 52, May, p. 48-58.

17. Gadgil, D.R. (1959), Origining of Modern Business Class--An Interim Report, Institute of Pacific Relations, New York.

18. Guha, Amalendy (1969), "Parsi Seths as Entrepreneurs, 1750-1850", Economic and Political Weekly 5, 29th August 1970, p.107 and " The Comprador Role of Parsi Seths, 1750-1850", Economic and Political Weekly 5, 28 November, 1970, 1933-1936 (The Parsis, followers of Zoraster who migrated from Iran to Western India 1300 years ago, have no basic roots in the country). Medhore "Entrepreneurship in India", Political Science Quarterly, 80 No.4, September, 1965, p.564. Timberg Thomas A., Industrial Entrepreneurship among the Trading Communities of Indial. How the Pattern Differs, Centre for International Affairs, Development Advisory Service, Economic Development Report, No. 136, Harvard University, July.

19. John Kenneth Galbraith (1969), "Economic Development", Harvard University Pres, Cambridge.

20. Kusum Nayar; Blossoms in the Dust (1973), 1962 (Quoted from Ram K. Vepa, Entrepreneurship for Development of Backward Areas, National Productivity council, New Delhi, p.21).

21. David C. Mc Clelland (1967), The Achieving Society, The Free Press, New York, p.43.

22. David C. McClelland (1966), "The Impulse to Modernization" in Modernization, The Dynamics of Growth, Myran Weiner (Ed.,) Voice of America Forum Lecturers, Voice of America, Washington D.C., p. 29-40.

23. Ram K. Vepa (1973), Entrepreneurship for Development of Backward Areas, National Productivity Council, New Delhi, p. 25.

24. Ram K Vepa, *op. cit.*, p.24.

25. With the help of sponsors, a group of students generally about a dozen, form themselves into a company and then select their own officers and Board of Directors. Since the company will operate for only a year, the products they select are usually easily made such as perfume, Jewellery, Toys or Christmas decorations. Quite after the product was allied to that of its sponsoring "big brother "company. The money required for operations was raised by each member by selling stock at 50 percent per share, usually, such shares were sold to adults in the community who were interested in the experiments, but a dividend was declared if the venture succeeds. The students buy their raw materials, manufacture, and sell their products in the open market. At the end of the year a share holder's report is prepared and the company dissolves itself, Ibid., p. 24-25.

26. Gangadhara Rao N. (1978), "Entrepreneurship in Industrial Estates; A Study With Special Reference to Coastal Andhra", p.176.

27. Mathew, J., Manimala (1999), Entrepreneurial Policies and Strategies, SAGE Publications, New Delhi also see, Venkata Rao, B.S, 1975 A Multidimensional Approach to Development of Entrepreneurship ; Significance of Training and others inputs, SIET . p.18, kanitkar, A. 1994 Integrating the Extension Approach in Entrepreneurial Development Activities; A Rational Experiences and Issues, SEDME, Vol.21. p. 1-19; Sage Gary, 1993, Entrepreneurship as an Development Strategy, Economic Development Review, Vol. 2, No.2, p.66-67, Mackenzie, Lynnryan. 1992 Fostering Entrepreneurship as a Rural Economic Development Strategy. Economic Development Review,

Vol.10, No. 4, p.38-44 and Covin J.G and Steven D.P.1991. A Conceptual Model of Entrepreneurship, Entrepreneurship Theory, Vol. 16, No. 1, p.7-25.

28. Ruddar Datt and Sundheram, K.P.M. (2006), "Indian Economy" S.Chand Publications, New Delhi, p.265.
29. Stigilitz, Joseph E. (2002b), "Globalization and Its Discontents", W.W. Norton & Company, VSA, p.9.
30. Bhagwati, Jagdish (2004), "In Defence of Globalization" Oxford University Press, New Delhi, p.3.
31. Neelam Jain (2004), "Small Scale Industries in the New Millenarian", Sedme, March, p.64-69.
32. Watanabe, Susumu (1970), Entrepreneurship in Small Enterprises in Japanese Manufacturing, International Labour Review, Vol. 102, No. 6, December, p.546.
33. A Pretty Fair Picture of the "Ruthlessly Democratic" Competition in the Japanese School System was given in The Times (London), 10th March, 1970, p.10.

6

FINDINGS AND SUGGESTIONS

Entrepreneur, the central figure of economic activity and propeller of progress, plays a crucial role in determining the level of development in any economy. The difference in the nature and magnitude of investment between the developed and underdeveloped countries and between different stages in the progress of any single country, is to be found in the size, energy, initiative and scope of operation of the entrepreneurial class. This reveals unmistakably their need, particularly in developing economies like India. This does not mean that these countries require immediately Schumpeter's innovating entrepreneur, the most vigorous of all entrepreneurs. The Schumpeterian entrepreneur is a rare species and it is rather difficult to get such enterprise. In fact these countries primarily need, innovators and the "imitators" or adaptors of technologies and products of developed countries who, even in Schumpeter's system are primarily responsible for transforming the countries into a magnitude of economic importance. The importance of such humbler entrepreneurs who "exploit possibilities as they present themselves and mostly on a small scale" must not be underestimated in developing economies. The enterprises may be small and unimpressive judged by the standards of more developed countries. But their success points the way for others and given the high propensity to imitate, which exists in a less developed area, can set in motion the "chain – reaction" which leads to cumulative progress.

Realizing this and based on sound economic reasons, the newly industrializing countries are placing great stress in their economic planning on the development of small and medium scale enterprises. India is no exception and rightly, the encouragement of small and medium scale industry has become a corner stone of her economic policy.

The present study relates to such of those entrepreneurs and their enterprises operating in Nellore district of Andhra Pradesh. Evaluation of entrepreneurship constitutes the core of the study.

NEED FOR THE STUDY

Entrepreneurship helps in the industrialization of the country in different ways viz., assembling and harnessing the various inputs, bearing the risks, innovating and imitating the techniques of production to reduce the cost and increase the quality and quantity, expanding the horizons of the market and coordinating and managing the manufacturing unit at various levels. In fact, the industrial development of a country crucially depends upon the number and abilities of its entrepreneurs. Entrepreneurship, therefore, is regarded as one of the determining factors of the industrial growth of a country.

The problem of underdevelopment has different dimensions in the different parts of India. This problem becomes still more complex in the backward districts like Nellore. Nellore is one of the industrially backward districts of the state of Andhra Pradesh, placed under the 'C' category by the Central Government inspite of its proximity to the industrial belt of Chennai and availability of railway heads, 180kms of national highways, power etc., the district has lagged behind in industrial development. The Nellore municipality was upgraded as a corporation by the Government of Andhra Pradesh on 8th October, 2004.

Therefore, the need to support the development of small scale entrepreneurship is more in case of units established in the backward regions than those coming up in the advanced regions of the country. Nellore district is such a backward region that needs special study for the policy formulation that will enable the district to grow industrially.

STATEMENT OF THE PROBLEM

In spite of the fact that small scale entrepreneurship has a long history of development and its importance in national economic scene is steadily growing, there is very little literature providing an objective assessment of small scale entrepreneurship. The literature available is mostly government reports, and more often than not studies by administration involved in formulation of policies for its implementation. This kind of literature is likely to lack objectivity and impartial assessment of the role of small scale entrepreneurship in the country.

This observation is more relevant in the context of small scale entrepreneurship in the district of Nellore, whose exact place of importance in the overall economic system and the direction of growth are not properly assessed. In view of the fact, that small scale entrepreneurship has come to occupy a pivotal rôle, a study about the nature of entrepreneurship, development trends in terms of number of units, employment and investment, incentives and assistance, besides financial; may be meaningful and purposive. The study, to begin with, analyses the growth and developmental factors of this sector over certain period, the factors responsible for entrepreneurial motivation, opinion of entrepreneurs regarding impact of globalization and liberalization on the small scale entrepreneurship. With this analysis, an attempt is made to identify their problems which would go a long way in helping suggest the future policies and remove hurdles restraining their growth and development.

OBJECTIVES OF THE STUDY

The objectives of the study are

1. To find out the socio-economic characteristics of entrepreneurs.

2. To probe the factors that motivated the entrepreneurs.
3. To ascertain the factors that contribute to the growth of entrepreneurship.
4. To study the impact of globalization and liberalization on the growth of entrepreneurship.
5. To identify the problems faced by entrepreneurs.
6. To give suggestions to promote entrepreneurship.

METHODOLOGY AND SAMPLING

Data is collected from primary and secondary sources. A pilot study was conducted to test comprehensiveness and validity of the questionnaire among selected enterprises and based on the responses obtained, necessary changes were made in the final Questionnaires.

Out of 653 Small Scale Enterprises, 30 % percent of the population was considered to determine the sample size. The sample units were selected randomly resulting in a sample size of 196 units. While selecting the sample units, the following sample frame work is considered.

1. The Small Scale Enterprises located in four Industrial Estates in Nellore (Andhra Pradesh Industrial Estate, Wood Complex, Auto nagar phase I, Auto nagar phase II), Industrial Estate, Gudur; Industrial Estate, Kavali; Industrial Developing Area, Pannemgedu; Integrated Industries Development Centre, Tada and Industrial Developing Area, Venkatachalam developed by state development agencies such as Andhra Pradesh Industrial Infrastructural Corporation (APIIC) and District Industries Centre (DIC) were considered for target population, as these are modern small scale enterprises.
2. The units having a capital investment (initial) of Rs. 1, 00,000 and above were considered.
3. The manufacturing units were only selected for the study.

4. The units which were started before 2001 and working currently were considered.
5. Sick and closed units were excluded, because of difficulty in obtaining relevant data.

The researcher consulted the annual reports of National Institute of Small Industry Extension Training (NISIET), Hyderabad, District Industries Centre, Nellore and Andhra Pradesh Industrial Infrastructural Corporation (APIIC), Nellore. For literature, the researcher had gone through various books, Census of Small Scale Industries, Economic Survey, Report on Small Enterprises (Abid Hussain Committee), Bulletins of Reserve Bank of India, journals, research reports, magazines, websites, manuals and newspapers on small scale industry and Entrepreneurship available in the libraries of the Department of Management studies, Sri Venkateswara University, Tirupathi, Indian Institute of Management, Bangalore, Sri Krishnadevaraya University, Ananthapur, Madras University, Chennai and Osmania University, Hyderabad.

SCOPE AND LIMITATIONS OF THE STUDY

The limitations of this study are as follows

1. The study has included the industries in industrial estates only, certain traditional industries located outside the industrial estate such as fisheries, aquaculture, beedi manufacture (a tobacco based industry), small cashew processing units, tile manufacturing units, ice and cold storage plants etc., were excluded.
2. Most of the entrepreneurs were not interested to disclose the financial data.

FINDINGS

It is proposed here to bring about a birds eye view of small scale entrepreneurship in Nellore district. The empirical findings of the study are presented.

A Profile of Socio–Economic Factors of Entrepreneurs

Ownership: Proprietary type of ownership was prominent amongst the respondents units, followed by partnership. In proprietary type of units, the owner-managers were sole-proprietary and had to attend to all the managerial tasks and routine operational tasks single handedly.

Age: The mean age (44.9 percent) of the entrepreneurs of Nellore district was between 26 to 35 years, and about 36.7 percent were in the age group of 36 to 50 years. However the young entrepreneurs (below 25years) were sole proprietors of their enterprises.

Educational Level: It is heartening to note, 50 percent of the entrepreneurs were graduates irrespective of their sex. 53.7 percent of graduates were below 25 years. The enterprises managed by the graduates were proprietary concern.

Caste: The entrepreneurship in Nellore district was dominated by forward caste (44.4 percent) followed by backward castes (39.8 percent) and scheduled caste and scheduled tribes (15.8 percent) . About 15.8 percent entrepreneurs belonged to scheduled caste and scheduled tribes. The graduate entrepreneurs (88 percent) belonged to forward caste and backward caste and are sole proprietors of their enterprises. However, majority of the entrepreneurs inspite of different castes were middle-aged (26 to 35 years). Coming to gender, 83.90 percent of male entrepreneurs belonged to forward caste. It is heartening to note that the good number of women (35.90 percent) from less privileged castes were motivated to start the enterprises of their own along with men.

The foregoing analysis shows that the entry into business activity was mostly confined to certain castes as in the case of other regions of the country. A few castes penetrating into entrepreneurial activities were also a phenomenon of the Nellore district. The entry of entrepreneurs from scheduled caste and scheduled tribe amply proves that the hold of caste structure on occupations in India is getting loosened throwing the doors of entrepreneurial opportunities wide open to people who are willing to take risks irrespective of their caste origins. This study evidences a great awakening among the under-privileged castes. This sort of entrepreneurial change is expected to accelerate the rate of wide spread and broad-based economic growth.

The experience of the developing countries shows that natural resources, capital, manpower and available technology and techniques, cannot guarantee entrepreneurial development without people's motivation. The relative measure of prosperity of different countries and regions is mostly a consequence of the relative abundance or scarcity of well motivated entrepreneurs of different sections of the community. The successful entrepreneurs have to come from various regions, strata of society and from various communities.

Family Background: The magnitude of entrepreneur's activity depends on the economic status of his father. It was observed that only 33.7 percent of entrepreneurs' fathers belonged to business families engaged in manufacturing or service industries and 62.8 percent of them were not having basic education. The average annual income of 41.3 percent of respondent's fathers was less than Rs. 75, 000 per annum. This leads to the conclusion that two thirds of entrepreneurs were first generation entrepreneurs.

The above trend demonstrates that the economic status has been increasing from generation to generation irrespective of their caste. This elevation leads to the increased entrepreneurial activity, breeding new class of entrepreneurs.

Economic Status: 46.4 percent of the entrepreneurs in the age group 26 to 35 years were earning between Rs 1,00,001 to Rs 5,00,000. 35.6 percent of partnership forms were earning more than Rs 5,00,000 per annum. The earnings of backward caste entrepreneurs were less than Rs 5,00,000 per annum. 44.4 percent of schedule caste entrepreneurs were among those entrepreneurs whose income was less than Rs.1,00,000 per annum. It could be interfered from above government concessions and reservation did not largely motivate the less privileged communities to venture into the entrepreneurship.

These findings suggest that the Indian society is witnessing a slow and gradual but sure transformation and the seeds of entrepreneurship are sprouting even in hitherto less enterprising social segments. Nevertheless, entrepreneurship is still largely confined to the communities that enjoyed a higher social status. Keeping this in view, much more stimulating environment must be created for the speedier dispersal of entrepreneurship even among all the remote segments of society.

MOTIVATIONAL FACTORS

Entrepreneur's ambitions, prime motives, facilitating factors, compulsions, sources of initial capital and reasons for choosing the particular place were also enquired into.

Motives: Ambitions or aspirations motivate men, activate them, broaden their vision and make the life meaningful. Ambition is an index of ones' own resourcefulness. Well conceived notions, careful planning, calculated risk-taking, timely decision-making and swift execution make the ambition-meaningful and fruitful. 30.1 percent of the entrepreneurs have started the enterprises to get self employed where as 27 percent wanted to continue the family business. 23 percent of them dissatisfied with the present job, have ventured into the business. However, only 15.8 percent were lured into business to make money.

Persons Influenced to Start the Enterprise: Among the factors, facilitating the emergence of entrepreneurship, the family members, friends, relatives and others played an important role in giving shape to entrepreneur's ambitions. About half of entrepreneurs (58.7 percent) have support from their family members to start own ventures.

Initial Source of Finance: The finances towards initial capital were encouragement mostly provided by family members. 41.8 percent of the entrepreneurs raised finance from family members and

35.7 percent from commercial banks. This indicates the confidence of the family in the capabilities of entrepreneur on the one hand and on the other hand the preparedness of the family to risk its savings in an entrepreneurial activity. On the top of these, the family support is a torch bearer in shaping the entrepreneur's new careers.

Training Programmes: Training and experience instil the confidence among the youth and serve as the nursery for building enterprises and accelerates the process of germination of entrepreneurship. Only 20.9 percent of the entrepreneurs attended the training programmes before starting their enterprises and mostly were trained by their family members. A majority (79.1 percent) of the entrepreneurs of Nellore district was not aware of the training programmes and the government agencies failed to create awareness about importance of the training programmes among the budding entrepreneurs.

Government Assistance: Government played a vital role in helping the entrepreneurs by providing financial support and other infrastructural facilities. 68.9 percent of the entrepreneurs availed government assistance in the form of financial support, marketing of products, procurement of raw material and to locate enterprise.

Place of Activity: The infrastructure facilities offered by the place in terms of raw material, labour, transport facilities and its proximity to the developing towns or cities attracts and stimulated the spirit of entrepreneurship. 37.8 percent of the entrepreneur's selected Nellore district due to the availability of resources at lesser cost and 36.8 percent selected due to the availability of raw materials. But 13.3 percent of entrepreneurs located their enterprises because of the home town, nearness to market and availability of the own plot.

GROWTH FACTORS

The socio-economic profile of the entrepreneurs and the motivational factors, presented above, provides many insights into the phenomenon of entrepreneurship in Nellore district.

However, on the basis of further exploration into the phenomenon of entrepreneurship the following findings have been obtained.

Investment in Enterprise: An attempt is made to measure the growth of the enterprises on the basis of the changes in investment between initial and the latest years. Initial year refers to the year of commencement and the latest year to the year of the survey(2004). The number of units with an investment more than 7 lakhs increased from 55 units to 91 units where as number of units with an investment less than 6 lakhs decreased from 141 to 85 units. It indicated that the units with less investment had graduated to large investment in the later year.

Initially every entrepreneur has to procure some finance of his/her own or loan from outside for the establishment of an enterprise. 77 percent of the entrepreneurs have taken loan for initial investment from financial institutions and commercial banks. Having borrowed money from the financial institutions and commercial banks, entrepreneurs have to maintain its credit worthiness by repaying the loan with interest. 72.8 percent of entrepreneurs have never defaulted in repayment of the loan. It indicates that entrepreneurs repay their loan very regularly and this explodes the myth relating to the low credit worthiness of small scale industry borrowers.

Government Subsidies and Incentives: The government of India and the government of Andhra Pradesh have been offering different types of incentives and subsidies to small scale enterprises. About half (52 percent) of the entrepreneurs are aware of subsidies and incentives available for their industry. The government has to create awareness among the prospective entrepreneurs about various incentives, subsidies and schemes available for them.

Employment: The growth of an enterprise was assessed on the basis of employment between the initial and latest years. Initially 58.26 percent of units employed less than 10 persons, decreased to 47.9 percent in the later years and the percentage of units employing more than 20 increased from 5.1 percent to 13.4 percent which was an indicator of growth of small scale units by providing more employment.

Training to Employees: The enterprise has to provide training to its employees in order to increase their performance level. 67.9 percent of the entrepreneurs did not provide any training to their employees and only 32.1 percent of entrepreneurs provided training to their employees. The entrepreneurs of small scale enterprises of Nellore district were not able to give importance to training programmes.

Profits: Profit is one of the conditioning factors for assessing the performance of the small enterprise. Nearly half of the entrepreneurs (46.9 percent) earned profit within the first year of commencement and only 3.6 percent of entrepreneurs started earning profits during the fourth and fifth years. But 76 percent of entrepreneurs reported that there was no change in profits during the last three years and 51 percent of entrepreneurs did not reinvest their profit in the firm. Further, they are in the process of diversifying into another business, investing in share market and diverting the money into unproductive assets like house construction, jewellory etc.,

Sales: The profitability of the firm depends upon its sales. Growth in the sales is an appropriate indicator of performance. Nearly three fourth (77 percent) of the entrepreneurs reported constant sales during the last three years and only 8.7 percent reported an increase in sales. It indicates that the small enterprises have remained stagnant since insignificant number of enterprises registered increase in profits and sales.

Advertising: Advertising plays a very important role today. It is a powerful promotional tool used by businesses and non business organizations for informing, persuading and reminding their targeted audiences. Here 63.3 percent of the entrepreneurs did not advertise their products and only 36.7 percent advertised their products in newspapers, pamphlets and local cable network. The entrepreneurs of Nellore district were not able to understand the importance of advertising which resulted in stagnant sales and profits.

IMPACT OF GLOBALIZATION AND LIBERALIZATION

In order to examine, the impact of globalization and liberalization on the growth of small scale enterprises, an attempt is made to study opinions of entrepreneurs regarding this. 87.8 percent mentioned that globalization and liberalization did not affect the products of enterprise.

Globalization and liberalization have brought many changes in economy in India. Entrepreneurs undeniably do have to experience stress and challenges at the work place and at outside as well. Entrepreneurs mentioned that globalization and liberalization have increased the promotional expenditure (Ist rank) followed by quality consciousness (2 nd rank) and threat from multi national companies (3rd rank).

MAJOR PROBLEMS ENCOUNTERED BY ENTREPRENEURS

Major Problems: The multifarious problems faced by small scale entrepreneurs are universal in character and interlinked with one other. Entrepreneurs confronted with high prices (mean 8.91) of raw materials, competition from small industries(mean 9.17), absenteeism (mean 8.53), shortage of fixed capital (mean 8.44), uncertainty of power (mean 4.56) and ineffective consultancy service provided by government (mean 7.38).

Complaint to Government Agencies: Having analyzed the problems of entrepreneurs, it is now to study whether they made any complaint to government agencies or not. Majority (90.3 percent) of the entrepreneurs did not make any complaint to government agencies and only 9.7 percent made a complaint. Out of which insignificant number (5 out of 19) received the response. It clearly shows apathy of the government agencies towards the problems faced by entrepreneurs.

ENTREPRENEURIAL OPINIONS OF SUCCESS

Entrepreneurial Success Factors and Expectations from Government: An important aspect of the study was to know, the opinion of entrepreneurs about the factors that contributed to their success. Entrepreneurs felt that moral support from family members and friends (Ist rank) was an important factor for the success. The timely assistance from the government and own property were the next important factors (2nd and 3rd ranks) for the success. The entrepreneurs expected the government to help in exporting their products, control the labour organization and treat all the entrepreneurs equally with out any bias and nepotism.

Aspirations about their Children: It is intended to examine whether entrepreneurs under study were interested in grooming their children as entrepreneurs of tomorrow. Majority (87.2 percent) of the entrepreneurs did not wish their children to become entrepreneurs but wanted their children to join a profession of their liking, engineers, government jobs and doctors. Only 12.8 percent of entrepreneurs were interested in seeing their sons/daughters as entrepreneurs.

Factors for Failure: It is equally important to know the factors that have contributed to the failure. Entrepreneurs expressed the lack of planning (Ist rank) was an important factor for failure, followed by having interest in more than one business(2nd rank), participation in politics (3rd rank) and expansion of business quickly (4th rank) are the factors in the descending role for failure.

Entrepreneurs Satisfaction about their Present Line of Business and Future Plans: An attempt is made to measure the entrepreneurs' satisfaction about their present line of business. Over half (57.2 percent) of the entrepreneurs were not satisfied with the present line of business and wanted to go for new business and change the product line. Only 42.8 percent were satisfied with the present line of business and wanted to expand the existing business.

SUGGESTIONS

On the basis of the above mentioned findings, we put forth some valuable and concrete suggestions for the growth and development of entrepreneurship in the backward region of Nellore district.

1. This study leads to the understanding that entrepreneurship should be looked upon as a skill which can be developed and cultivated. The study also leads to the understanding, that promotion of entrepreneurship involves inputs or facilitation at various levels and over a period of time. Families, and specially the parents, need to be sensitized about gender-bias in child-rearing practices. They need to treat their sons and daughters equally and thus to promote achievement-motivation and self-confidence in children of both sexes. The parents must encourage the girl children to become entrepreneurs along with the male children.

2. The educational system throughout its various levels, needs to encourage the children to develop good communication ability, self confidence and other skills. Case studies of successful entrepreneurs and periodic face to face interaction with persons who have distinguished themselves as successful entrepreneurs may go a long way in preparing the children for entrepreneurship. At the secondary or high school and junior college level, other basic skills like preparing projects, writing project reports, writing business plans etc. may be imparted. A network of agencies/institutions, both Governmental and Non–Governmental, providing a variety of services to promote and support entrepreneurship is very important. Several such agencies are in existence and are doing good work. However, these agencies can become more meaningful and more effective if the foundations of entrepreneurship are laid at the level of family and the educational institutions.

3. Further, in the present context, Entrepreneurship Development programmes could be more pro–active, broad–based (in terms of target group) and of a continuous nature. Along with all this, efforts also need to be made at various levels to create and promote societal attitudes which approve of and facilitate entrepreneurship. The success stories of entrepreneurship among those who have not even completed high school are to be put in front of graduates to instil confidence. Success stories not only generate entrepreneurship but also improve its quality. Entrepreneurs should not be blamed for all the ills of business houses, big or small. Blaming the entrepreneurship every now and then for the lapse of administration leads to the impression that entrepreneurship itself is something unethical or anti-social. If the youth of the nation are given such an impression of the entrepreneurs, it cannot help the germination of seeds of enterprise from among the youth. It is the responsibility of the state, the political parties not to indulge in the past time of such mudslinging for the good and healthy growth of the entrepreneurship.
4. The Nellore district being predominantly agricultural, has vast potentialities for the setting up of multifarious agro–based industries like flour mills, animal feeds, rice, oil and dhal mills, confectionary, solvent plants, straw mills, seed factories, agricultural tools and equipments etc.
5. The important dominant caste in the field of entrepreneurship in Nellore district was forward caste (44.4 percent) followed by backward castes (39.8 percent). The government agencies at central and state level should encourage scheduled caste and scheduled tribe young graduates for entrepreneurship. Moreover, various incentives, schemes, facilities and subsidies available for them should be advertised.

6. Despite good number of schemes and programmes launched by the state, the Nellore district continues to be a backward region because the incentives channelised through multifarious agencies, have failed to bear the desired fruits. Hence, there is need for co-ordination among various government and non–government agencies to avoid multiplicity and overlapping of activities.
7. Majority of small scale entrepreneurs, who were assisted by different developmental and financial institutions, belonged to the affluent, resourceful and politically influential people. It is therefore, suggested that working of these agencies/institutions should be so improved and consolidated that really deserving and financially weak but technologically sound enterprises get priority over bigger and financially sound yet ' small scale units'.
8. For developing and inculcating entrepreneurial talent among the people, besides Entrepreneurial Development Programme (EDP), government may use media slogans like : "*Be an entrepreneur and serve the nation*", "*Be the master and not the servant* " *etc.*,
9. Small scale enterprises are dispersed across the country in urban, semi–urban as well as in rural areas. The products/services offered by them also are diverse. The government, financial institutions and other non–government organizations have to start independent consultancy agencies. The proposed agency would identify entrepreneurial needs, opportunities and issue certificates to eligible person as "Certified Small Scale Entrepreneur" after completion of proper training in entrepreneurship.
10. The Government, State Financial Corporations, Technical Consultancy Organisation, Small Industries Development Bank of India and Industry Associations should update

their websites with their schemes and concessions for small scale enterprises periodically.

11. One of the problems faced by small enterprises is lack of marketing information and marketing of products. The government and other agencies have to provide this information through database in internet. The database could be organized through established institutes and market research firms.
12. As per the findings of the study, there is a potential for technical and managerial assistances for enterprises. For this, engineering colleges, management institutes and universities can take advantage of this opportunity to provide technical and managerial consultancy to local small enterprises. Initiatives from retired professionals could also be considered for this purpose.
13. The District Industries Centre, Department of Industries and Commerce, local industry associations and banks play an important role in solving the problems of small enterprises by developing local advisory boards, to deliberate on problems and improvements of small enterprises and finally advise or recommend or decide the remedial measures expeditiously.
14. As per the findings of the study, most of small scale enterprises have constant sales and profits from last three years. It was advisable to the District Industries Centre and other financial institutions should provide training, seminars, workshops and conferences for 3 to 5 days in which all government officials, expert persons and entrepreneurs come together to offer suggestions to solve their problems directly by face to face contact.
15. It is heartening to note that a sense of general awareness is dawning among the masses, about the virtues of self-employment through industrial entrepreneurship. Thus,

the artisan and factory workers should be awakened, activated and brought into the fold of entrepreneurial class.

16. The Central and State agencies should advertise the advantages and benefits of globalization and liberalization to the small scale entrepreneurs by conducting public meetings, conferences and seminars. The educational institutes, colleges and universities have to encourage young graduates and post graduates to participate in them and develop entrepreneurship among them.
17. Further, in order to deal with complaints of entrepreneurs the District Industries Centres and the Directorate of Industries have to appoint a specialized staff to operate these activities and to have quick results.
18. Finally, paucity of statistical data is another serious handicap. For example, the Directorate of Industries, being the nodal organization and whose purpose is to carry out the developmental activities, does not keep records on production of different items within this sector. The lack of a systematic data also stands in the way of a proper assessment of the impact of the government schemes on the small scale units. Therefore, the government has to take serious efforts to build up an accurate and reliable data base, covering the various aspects of small sector, not only in Nellore district, but also in all the districts of Andhra Pradesh and also in all the states. In order to achieve this, what is needed, is the strict adherence to the already existing "Registration–cum–collection of statistics schemes" which was introduced as early in 1959.

Further, it would be purposeful to decentralize the development policy decisions and assistance programmes for small enterprise. As suggested above, the local industry associations of small enterprises and banks could be empowered to recommend

/decide on all problems faced by small enterprises in the region. It is expected that these suggestions, when implemented could lead to growth and development of small scale enterprise.

DIRECTIONS FOR FUTURE RESEARCH

While doing the research, the researcher observed some areas, which need to be researched. The results of this research study encourage several directions for future research. Scope for further research in the following areas has been suggested:

1. The scope for growth and development of entrepreneurship is as wide as discussed in the study. This growth may vary depending upon the nature of enterprise and the type of industry. A further study is suggested to examine the impact of the nature of industry and growth and development of entrepreneurship.
2. As noted in the study, most of the small enterprises were proprietary firms. Depending on ownership pattern i.e., proprietary, partnership and others, further study could be initiated to compare the performances based on ownership patterns.
3. An indepth study on problems of an enterprise and the type of government interventions could be an interesting area for future research.
4. A further study on measurement of performance and success-failure parameters of small enterprises is suggested. The performance parameters are difficult to measure, and under Indian conditions developing suitable measures is very important.
5. The results of the study show that, the perception of owner-managers in use of government assistance is negative. The reasons need to be found out by further studies. Studies on alternative modes such as counselling, mentoring and networking efforts could be initiated.

Future research on these suggested topics could be initiated on regional basis or across the country. It is expected that future studies in such important areas would contribute significantly to the growth and development of small scale enterprises. The ultimate objective would be to achieve a sustainable growth and development of small scale enterprises.

BIBLIOGRAPHY

A Pretty Fair Picture of the "Ruthlessly Democratic" competition in the Japanese school system was given in The Times ,London, 10 March, 1970.

Adam Smith specifically included the acquired and useful abilities of all the inhabitants or the members of the society in his concept of capital. (An enquiry into the nature and causes the Wealth of Nations, Common Ed., Random House Inc., 1937, Book II).

Ahluwalia.I.J " Industrial Policy and Industrial Performance in India", Lucas & D.Robert and Papanek F.Gustav,Ed.The Indian Economy, Delhi: Oxford University Press, 1998.

Akhouri M.M.P, "Entrepreneurship and Small Industry Development-Experience form Asian Region" in the proceedings of the workshop 'Entrepreneurship and Small Enterprise Development: Policies and Strategies; Kingston, Jamaica, 26-30 March, 1990.

Alec, P.Alexander, Greek Industrialists, An Economic and Social Analysis, Centre of Planning and Economic Research, Athens, 1964.

Alexander.A.P., Greek Industrialists-An Economic and Social Analysis, Center of Planning and Economic Research, Athens,1961.

Alfred Marshall emphasized the importance of education "as a national investment" and in his view the most valuable of all of capital is that invested in human beings, Principles of Economics, 8 th ed., Mac Millian, 1930.

Altaf.Zafar, Pakistani Entrepreneurs-Their Development Characteristics and Altitudes, IBD Publishers and Distributors, New Delhi.1984.

Amlendu Guha, " Parsi Seths and Entrepreneurs, 1750-1850", Economic and Political Weekly, Aug.29, 1970,and " The Comprador Role of Parsi Seths, 1750-1850", *Economic and Political Weekly*, Nov. 28, 1970.

Andhra Pradesh Year Book, 2003-2004, Government of Andhra Pradesh, Vol.I, Hyderabad, 2004.

Andhra Pradesh Year Book, 2003-2004, Government of Andhra Pradesh, Vol.II, Hyderabad, 2004.

Andrew, F. Brimmer, The Settings of Entrepreneurship in India", *The Quarterly Journal of Economics*, Nov.1955.

Anitha, H.S., Laxmishra, A.S., Women Entrepreneurship in Inida, *Southern Economist*, Vol. 38, No. 4, June, 1999.

Arun Joshi, Lala Shri Ram: A Study in Entrepreneurship & Industrial Management, Orient Longman, New Delhi, 1975.

Ashis Gupta, "Indian Entrepreneurial Culture: Bengal and Eastern India" in 'The Culture of Entrepreneurship 'Ed.by Brigitte Berger, The Tata McGraw-Hill publishing Company Ltd., New Delhi, 1992.

Ashis Nandy and Raymond L. Owvens, The New Vysyas, Allied Publishers Pvt., Ltd, 1977.

Atkins, M H and Lowe, J F., Sizing Up Small Firm : UK and Australian Experience, *International Small Business Journal*, 15(3), 1997.

Ayala Malach-pines, Dov Dvir, Arik Sadeh, "The Making of Israeli High-Technology Entrepreneurs: An Explanatory Study" *The Journal of Entrepreneurship*, Sage Publications, New Delhi, January-June, 2004.

Bala Subrahmanya, M.H, Mathirajan, M and Balachandra.P, 'R & D Behaviour Objectives and Performance of Small Scale Industries in Karnataka' *Sedme*, Vol.29, No.1, March, 2002.

Bala Subrahmanya, M.H., 'Technological Innovations in Small Enterprises: Comparative Study of Bangalore and North-East England, *Economic and Political Weekly*, Vol.XXXVIII. No.21, May24-30, 2003.

Bellard, Anne-Marie, "The Role of Entrepreneurship in Reconstructing the Russian Economy", University of Nevade, Reno, 1997.

Benjamin Higgins, Economic Development, Central Book Depot, Allahabad, 1961.

Berna, J.J., Industrial Entrepreneurship in Madras State, Asia Publishing House, Bombay, 1960

Bert.F.Hoselitz, The Entrepreneurship Element in Economic Development, International Hand Book of Management, Mc Graw Hill, NewYork, 1965.

Bhagwati, Jagdish, " In Defence of Globalization" Oxford University Press, New Delhi, 2004.

Bhanushali.S.G., Entrepreneurship Development, An Interdisciplinary Approach, Himalaya Publication House, Bombay,1987.

Bhattacharya. S.N., Entrepreneurship Development in India and the South-East Asian Countries, Light and Life Publishers, New Delhi, 1979.

Bisht, N.S. et.al., Entrepreneurship Reflections and Investigations (Ed.)., Chugh Publication, Allahabad, 1989.

Boliko, Mbuli, "New Perspectives in Entrepreneurship and SME Development: A Human Resource Management Approach (Small Scale Enterprise, Medium Scale Enterprises), unpublished Ph.D, Nagoya University, Japan, 1996.

Bolton, B and Thomson, J, "Entrepreneurs Talent Temperament, Technique", Butterworth – Heinemann, Boston, 2000.

Burrows, R and Curran, J, Sociological Research on Service Sector Small Business: Some Conceptual Considerations Work, Employment and Society, 3(4), 1989.

Cas Feng Qi, "Entrepreneurial Managers in China's Enterprise Reforms," China Business Issue, 1995.

Census of India, Office of Registrar General & Census Commissioner, Series I, India, 2001.

Chachadi, A H, Decision Making in Small Industry, Unpublished doctoral thesis, Karnataka University, Dharwad, 1988.

Chandra R.K, Entrepreneurial Success: A Psychological Study, New Delhi: Sterling Publishers, 1991.

Chandrapoojary, Entrepreneurship Pull & Push Effect, *Sedme*, Vol.No. XXIV, September, 1999.

Chawla, A.S., Batra, G.S., and Dufatanye Jean d'Amour. ' Financing Practices and Problems of Small and Medium Enterprises in Rwande', *Sedme*, Vol.31, No.4, December, 2004.

Chitra Ramachandran, "Status of Women Entrepreneurs Who Established Micro Entrepreneurs in Madurai District" Unpublished Ph,D Madurai Kamaraj University, Madurai, 2005.

Chitra Rao and Mishra S.P, " Selection of Potential Entrepreneurs– An Appraisal of Methodologies", *Sedme*, Sept. 1985.

Clarence H.Danhof, Observations of Entrepreneurship in Agriculture and the Entrepreneurs, Harvard University Press, England 1949.

Covin J.G and Steven D.P., A Conceptual Model of Entrepreneurship, Entrepreneurship Theory, Vol. 16, No. 1. 1991.

Curran, James and Blackburn, R.A, Researching the Small Enterprise, Sage Publications : 1. London, 2001.

David C. Mc Clelland, The Achieving Society, The Free Press, New York, 1967.

David C. McClelland, "The Impulse to Modernization " in Modernization, The Dynamics of Growth, Myran Weiner (Ed.,) Voice of America Forum Lecturers, Voice of America, Washington D.C., 1966.

Deshpande M.U, Entrepreneurship of Small Scale Industries, Deep & Deep Publications, New Delhi, 1984.

E.Desingu Setty, " Promoting Small Entrepreneurship: Problems and Prospects" in 'Developing Entrepreneurship: Issues and Problems', SIET, Hyderabad, 1980.

Everett E.Hagen, The Economics of Development, Home Wood III : Richard D. Irwin, 1968.

Francis Walker, The Wages Question, Henry Holt, New York 1986.

Frederick, H, Entrepreneurial Organization: As a Factor in Economic Development, *Quarterly Journal of Economics*, Vol. LXX, No.3, Aug. 1956.

Gadgil D.r, The Industrial Evolution of India in Recent Times (1860-1939), Oxford University Press, London, 1959.

Gadgil, D.R., Origins of the Modern Indian Business Class-An Interim Report, International Secretariat, Institute of Pacific Relations, New York, 1959.

Gadgil, D.R., The Industrial Evolution of India in Recent Times: 1860-1939, Oxford University Press, Bombay, 1971.

Gaikwad.V.R., and Tripathy.R.N., Socio-Psychological Factors Influencing Industries Entrepreneurship in Rural Areas, National Institute of Community Development, Hyderabad,1970.

Gangadhara Rao.N., Entrepreneurship and Growth of Enterprise in Industrial Estates, Deep & Deep Publications, New Delhi,1986.

Geoffrey G. Meredith, Robert E. Nelson, Philip A Neck, " The Practice of Entrepreneurship", International Labour Office, Genera, 1982.

Gnana.Kannan, "Training for Entrepreneurship Development" in Development of Entrepreneurship Issues and Problems', SIET, Hyderabad, 1980.

Government of India, Economic Survey, 2002-2003, Statement 2.7, New Delhi, 2003.

Government of India, Planning Commission, Fourth Five Year Plan, 1969-74, Vol.II,1999.

Government of India, Planning Commission, Ninth Five Year Plan, 1997-2002, Vol.II, New Delhi, 1999.

Government of India, Planning Commission, Tenth Five Year Plan, 2002-2007, Vol.I, Annexure .3-A, New Delhi, 2003.

Government of India, Report of the Committee on Development of Small and Medium Entrepreneurs, Ministry of Industrial Development, New Delhi, 1975.

Guha, Amalendy, " The Comprador Role of Parsi Seths, 1750-1850", *Economic and Political Weekly* 5, 28 November, 1970, 1933-1936

Guha, Amalendy, "Parsi Seths as Entrepreneurs, 1750-1850", *Economic and Political Weekly* 5, 29 August 1970

Gupta, M.C., Entrepreneurship in Small Scale Industries, Anmol Publications, New Delhi, 1987.

Gustar, F. Papanek, "The Development of Entrepreneurship", American Economic Review, 52, May 1962.

Hadimani. R.N., Dynamics of Industrial Entrepreneurship, Ashish Publishing House, New Delhi, 1985.

Haksever, C, Total Quality Management in the Small Business Environment, Business Horizons 39 (2), 1996.

Hand Book of Statistics, Chief Planning Officer, Nellore, 2004.

Hanumantha Rao, K.S. and Sumithra, D.G., "Planning and the Growth of Industrial Entrepreneurship in India", *The Indian Journal of Commerce*, No.65, Dec., 1965.

Harris. John.R., "Nigerian Entrepreneurship," and Nigerian Entrepreneurship in Industry", in Kilby(ed) Entrepreneurship and Economic Development, The Free Press, New York,1971.

Harris. John.R.," Nigerian Entrepreneurship in Industry", in Growth and Development in Nigerian Economy (ed) Eicher and lied Biokes, East Lausin Michigan University Press,1970.

Hazlehurst, L.W., Entrepreneurship and the Merchant Caste in a Punjab City ., Durham, D.C, Duke University, Common Wealth Studies Center, 1966.

Heidman, Marine Faith, "Moving to Entrepreneurship : An Exploration of Midlife Executive Women's Perceptions of their Transition into New Ways of Working (Job loss, informal working), unpublished Ph.D, Michigan State University, 1997.

Helen, B Lamb, "The Rise of Indian Business Communities", Pacific Affairs, 23, No. 2., June 1955.

Hery, M.J, "Contrasting Factors in the Modernization of China and Japan", Simon Kaznets et al.(Eds)., Economic Growth: Brazil, India, Japan, N.C.Duke University Press, Dusham, 1965.

Higgins, Benjamin, Introduction to a Symposium on Entrepreneurship and Labour skills in Indonesian Economic Development, Yale University, South East Asia Studies, NewHavens,Conn.,1961.

Honig, Benson, "Human Capital and Structural Upheaval: A Study of Manufacturing Firms in the West Bank", *Journal of Business Venture*, Vol.16, No.6, Nov, 2001.

Howard Spodak, The Manchestrisation of Ahmedabad,*The Economic Weekly*, 17 (11), March 13, 1965.

Hozari, R.K., The Structure of Corporate Sector, Asia Publications House Bombay, 1965.

Huang, Xueli, Soutar, Geoffrey, N and Brown, Alan, 'New Product Development Processes in Small and Medium-sized Enterprises: Some Australian Evidence, *Journal of Small Management*, Vol.40, No.1, January, 2002.

James T. McCrory, Case Studies in Latent Industries Potential: Small Industry in a North Indian Town, Ministry of Commerce and Industry, Government of India, Delhi, 1956.

Jawahar.R.M.P, "Entrepreneurship Development in a Science Park", *Sedme*, Vol.20, No.3, September, 1994.

Jayachandran, G,Vijayalakhsmi,B., Hima Chalam.D., Entrepreneurial Profile in Industrial Estate A study, *Sedme*, Vol, XXIV, No.2, September, 1997.

John Kenneth Galbraith, "Economic Development", Harvard University Press, Cambridge, 1969.

John, J.Carroll, "The Philippino Manufacturing Entrepreneur: Agent and Product of Changes," Corroll University Press, ITHACO, 1965.

John, J.Carroll, The Philippine Manufacturing Entrepreneur: Agent and Product of Change, Corroll University Press, ITHACO,1965.

Joseph Alois Schumpeter, Business Cycle, Mc Graw Hill Book Company, New York, 1939.

Joseph Alois Schumpeter, The Theories of Economic Development, Translated by R.Opie Cambridge, Harvard University Press, 1934.

Jyotirmayee kar, "Credit, Demand and Supply: A Study of Small-Scale Units" *The Journal of Entrepreneurship*, Sage Publications, New Delhi, July, December, 2002.

Kalyani, W, Chandralekha, K., "Association between Socio-economic Demographic Profile and Involvement of Women Entrepreneurs in their Enterprise Management", *The Journal of Entrepreneurship*, Sage Publications, New Delhi, July – December, 2002.

Kamala Singh, "Women Entrepreneurs", Ashish Publishing House, New Delhi, 1992.

Kanitkar A, "Integrating the Extension Approach in Entrepreneurship Developing Activities: Rationale, Experience and Issues", *Sedme*, Vol.21, No.2, June ,1992.

Kanitkar, A. Integrating the Extension Approach in Entrepreneurial Development Activities; A Rational Experiences and Issues, *Sedme*, Vol.21.

Kasi Reddy, M, 'Profile of Scheduled Caste and Scheduled Tribe Entrepreneurs in Andhra Pradesh: An Empirical Study' , *Sedme*, Vol.30, No. 2, June 2003.

Kennedy. P., " Entrepreneurship in the Private and Public Sectors in China", Bulletin of Institute of Development Studies, Sussex, June, 1971.

Khanka S.S, Industrial Development of Backward Areas, Himalaya Publishing House, New Delhi,1994.

Khanka.S.S, Entrepreneurship in Small Scale Industries, Himalaya Publishing House, Bombay, 1990.

Kilby .Peter, Industrialization in a Open Economy, Nigeria, University Press, Cambridge.1969.

Kindleberger, "Economic Development," Mc Graw-Hill, New York, 1961.

Knight, H.Frank, Risk Uncertainty and Profit, Houghton Muffin Company, Chapter VII-XI, New York, 1957.

Krishna Kumar, Entrepreneurial Success: An Empirical Study in Mahaboob Nagar District, *Sedme,* Vol. XXV, 1997.

Kroef.J.M.Van Der, "Entrepreneurs and Middle Class in Indonesia", Economic Development and Cultural Change, Vol.2, 953-54.

Kusum Nayar; Blossoms in the Dust, 1962 (quoted from Ram K. Vepa, Entrepreneurship for Development of Backward Areas, National Productivity council, New Delhi, 1973).

Lakshamana Rao.V, Industrial Entrepreneurship in India, Chugh Publications, New Delhi,1986.

Lakshmane Rao. V, Industrial Entrepreneurship in India, Chugh Publications, Allahabad, 1986.

Landes, D.S, "French Entrepreneurship and Industrial Growth in the Ninteenth Century", *Journal of Economic History*, May,1949.

Li. Fang, "The Social Organization of Entrepreneurship: The Rise of Private Firms in China (Economic Reform)" unpublished Ph.D, University of Chicago, Chicago, 1997.

Lillian Vernonkatz, The Characteristics of a Successful Entrepreneur, *Journal of Economic Literature*, Vol.38, No.1, 1998.

Louks, Kenneth, Training Entrepreneurship for Small Business Creation: Lessons from experience. ILO Geveva, Oxford and IBH Publishing Co.Pvt.Ltd,1991.

Mackenzie, Lynnryan, Fostering Entrepreneurship as a Rural Economic Development Strategy, *Economic Development Review*, Vol.10, No. 4, 1992.

Madhu Murthy.K, "Some Aspects of Entrepreneurship Development in Developing Economics with specific reference to India, "Unpublished Ph.D Thesis, Kakatiya University, Warangal, 1997.

Manohar U. Deshpande, Entrepreneurship of Small Scale Industries, Deep and Deep Publications, New Delhi, 1982.

Manohar.U Deshpande, "Entrepreneurship of Small Industries-Concept, Growth and Management", Deep&Deep publications, New Delhi, 1982.

Mark Casson, "Enterprise and Leadership" Edwar and Wlgar Publication, UK., 2000.

Mathew, J., Manimala, Entrepreneurial Policies and Strategies, SAGE Publications, New Delhi 1999.

Mathew, P.W, "SME Package: Lingering Lacunae", The Hindu, August 15th 2005.

Medhore, "Entrepreneurship in India", *Political Science Quarterly*, 80 No. 4, September, 1965.

Merris. Peter, The Social Barriers to African Entrepreneurship, Institute for Development Studies, University College, Nairobi.

Mershall, A, Principle of Economics: An Introductory Volume, The English Language Book Society and MacMillan, London, 1961.

Miracle.M.,"Capitalism, Capital Markets and Competition in West Africa Trade" in Mellasoux .C., (ed) The Development of Indigenous Trade and Markets in West Africa, Oxford University Press, London.

Mitchell, B.C. "Motives of Entrepreneurs: A Case Study of South Africa", *The Journal of Entrepreneurship*, Sage Publications, New Delhi, July-December, 2004.

Mitra,D.K., Bhatia, G.S., Pannuselvam, R., Maryth Powel, " Training Methodology and Inputs for Micro, Small and Medium Scale Enterprise in UK.", *Sedme*, Vol. XXIV, No. 2 June, 1997.

Moulik, T.K., Patel and Basu, Rural Entrepreneurship, Center for Management in Agriculture, Indian Institute of Management, Ahmadabad, 1978.

Nafgiger, E. Wayne, "Relationship between Education and Entrepreneurship in Nigeris," *The Journal of Developing Areas*, Vol.4, No. 3, April,1970.

Nafziger, E.Wayne, "The Effect of the Nigerian Extended Family on Entrepreneurial Activity" Economic Development and Cultural Change, 18, No. 1 A.1 October, 1969.

Nafziger, E.Wayne, "The Relationship between Education and Entrepreneurship in Nigeria", *The Journal of Developing Areas*, 4th April, 1970.

Nafziger, E.Wayne, African capitalism, A Case Study in Nigerian Entrepreneurship, Hoover Institution, Standford, 1977.

Nafziger.F.W., Class, Caste and Entrepreneurship–A Study of Indian Industrialists, An East West Centre, The University Press of Hawali, Honululu, 1978.

Nagaraj.R, "Performance of India's Manufacturing Sector in the 1990s: Some Tentative Findings", Shuji Uchikawa(ed.,), Economic Reforms and Industrial Structure in India, Delhi, 2002.

Narasimha Murthy. B.E.V.V., Entrepreneurship in Small Towns, Mittal Publications, New Delhi, 1989.

Narendra S. Bisht and Pamila K. Sharma, Entrepreneurship: Expectations and Experience, Himalaya Publication House, Bombay, 1991.

Nayudamma, Y, "Convocation Address, First Annual Convocation on 7th May, Kakatiya University, Warangal, Andhra Pradesh, 1978.

Neelam Jain, "Small Scale Industries in the New Millenarian", *Sedme*, March, 2004.

Omoiele, M.Tambura, "African American Entrepreneurship: Socio-economic Factors Influencing Success and Failure", unpublished Ph.D, Union Institute, 1997.

Panda, N.M, ' Marketing Management in Small Service Enterprises: A case study of Hotel Industry in Nagaland', *Sedme,* Vol:30, No.2, June 2003.

Pannalal, "Status of Small Scale Enterprises in Industrial Estates in Andhra Pradesh: A Study", *Sedme,* Vol.21, No.4, Dec.,1994, New Delhi.

Papanek Gustav.F., Pakistan's Development Social Goals and Private Incentives, Harvard University Press, Cambridge, Massachusetts,1967.

Patel V.G,"Entrepreneurship Development Programs in India" in 'Development of New Entrepreneurs', EDII, Ahmedabad,1987.

Paul A. London, Merchants as promoters of Rural Development, An Indian Case Study, Praeger Publishers, New York, 1978.

Penrose E T, The Theory of Growth of the Firm, Blackwell, Oxford, 1959.

Peter F. Drucker, Innovation and Entrepreneurship Practice and Principles, Heienemann, London, 1985.

Peter Kilbly, "Hunting the Heffalump": Entrepreneurship and Economic Development (ed.,), The Free Press, New York, 1971.

Phansalkar, S J, How Not to Ruin Your Small Industry, Sage Publications, New Delhi, 1996.

Prabath, S.V., Entrepreneurship Development in India a Review, *Sedme,* Vol, XXIV, No. 3, September, 1997.

Prederick Harbinson, and Charles A. Myer, "Education, Manpower and Economic Growth," Oxford and 1BH Publishing Co, Calcutta, 1968.

Radha Shyam Rungta, " The Rise of Business Corporations in India", 1851–1900, Cambridge University Press, 1970.

Rajendran, G, 'A Study on the Entrepreneurial Development in Andaman and Nicobar Islands', *Sedme*, Vol.29, No.4, December, 2002.

Ram k. Vepa, Entrepreneurship for Development of Backward Areas, National Productivity Council, New Delhi, 1973.

Ranjeeth, Asthana,K. "Entrepreneurship Development", *Yojana*, Vol. 42, No.8, August, 1998.

Rao R. V, Indian Handicrafts, Bookhamas Private Limited, Hyderabad, 1969.

Ravi Chandra.K, "Entrepreneurial Success: A Psychological Study" Sterling Publishers Pvt, Ltd., New Delhi, 1991.

Ravi.K.Zutshi "Role of Technical Entrepreneurs in Industrial Development- An Alternative View" in Technical Entrepreneurship: Issues of Research &Application(Ed) Vinayshil Gautham, Global Business Press, New Delhi, 1992.

Resnik, P, The Small Business Bible: The Make or Break Factors Survival and Success, John Willey, New York, 1988.

Richard A. Peterson, Entrepreneurship and Economic Development, Vol. XII -2, 1962.

Richard. G. P. McMahon, 'Growth and Financial Profiles Amongst Manufacturing SMEs from Australia's Business Longitudinal Survey', Entrepreneurship: Theory and Practice, Vol.26, No.2, 2001.

Rolland Lebrasseur, Louis Zanibbi and Terrence J. Zinger, 'Growth Momentum in the Early Stages of Small Business Start-ups', *International Small Business Journal*, Vol.21, No.3, August, 2003.

Ruddar Datt and Sundharam K.P.M., "Indian Economy", S. Chand and Company Ltd., New Delhi, 2006.

Ruddar Datt and Sundheram, K.P.M, "Indian Economy" S.Chand Publications, New Delhi, 2006.

Sage Gary, Entrepreneurship as an Development Strategy, *Economic Development Review*, Vol. 2, No.2, 1993.

Sallappan R, Venkatapathy, R, Entrepreneurial Awareness and Practice among students , *Sedme*, Vol. XXV, No.2, June, 1998.

Sarangadharam.M and Razia Begum, "Women Entrepreneurship : Institutional Support and Problems, Discovery Publishing House, New Delhi, 1995.

Sarveswara Rao.B., and Lakshamana Rao.V., "Industrial and Commercial Entrepreneurship in the Coastal Region of Andhra Pradesh", ICSSR Research Abstracts Quarterly, Oct-Dec., 1978.

Say, J.B, "Catheism of Political Economy", London Sherwood, 1815.

SBA office of Advocacy, The Facts About Small Business, 1997..

Schatz.Sayre., The Capital Shortage Illusion, Government Spending in Nigerian, Oxford Unversity Press, 1965.

Selameab, Wolde Tsadik, "Factors Impacting Entrepreneurial Behaviour Among Graduates of Post-secondary Entrepreneurship Programme(Small Businesses)", University of Minnesote, 1997.

Service Area Credit Plan, Syndicate Bank, Lead District Office, Nellore, 2005.

Sharma, R.A., Entrepreneurial Change in Indian Industry, Sterling Publications Pvt., Ltd., New Delhi, 1980.

Sharma.S.V.S. "Characteristics of Entrepreneurs" in 'Development of Entrepreneurship Issues and Problems', SIET, Hyderabad, 1980.

Sharma.S.V.S.Small Entrepreneurial Development in Some Asian Counties- A Comparative Study, Light and Life Publishers, New Delhi, 1979.

Shravanvel.p, Entrepreneurial Development: Principles, Policies and Programmes, Ess-Pee-Kay Publishing House, Madras, 1987.

SIET, Socio-Psychological Factors Influencing and Adoption of the Innovation of Starting a Small Industry Unit, SIET Institute, Hyderabad, 1974..

Simon Kuznets has pointed out that measures of capital formation based on fixed capital are deficient because they omit expenditure for education, non–profit research, health, recreation etc, which "contributed to economic growth by increasing the efficiency of a complex productive system," (six lecturers on Economic Growth, The Free Press of Glencoe, New York, 1958).

Singh Pritam, The Role of Entrepreneurship in Economic Development: Issues and Policies, Butani and Singh (Ed), Vora and Co., Bombay, 1966.

Singh, P.N., Development Entrepreneurship for Economic Growth, Vikas Publishing House Pvt Ltd., New Delhi,1986.

Some Notes Towards a Theory of Derived Development in the Economics of Underdevelopment, Ed., A.N. Agrawala & S.P.Singh.

Stauworth, M.J.K and Curran, J. "Management Motivation in the Smaller Business, " A Gower Press special study, Essex, 1973.

Steek, Charles N, "Entrepreneurship, Institutions and Economic Growth", New York University, New York, 1997.

Stigilitz, Joseph E, "Globalization and Its Discontents", W.W. Norton & Company, VSA, 2002b.

Subbi Reddy, T and Sobha Reddy.N., Profile of Small Entrepreneurs in Kurnool, *Sedme*, Vol..XI, March, 1994.

Subbi Reddy. T and Appa Rao. P. B, Entrepreneurship Development Programme–An Evaluation of the Suitability of the Candidates Selected, (memeo), Pandu vennela prachuranahi, Anantapur, 1987.

Subramanian.R., ShivaKumar.K., and Palanisami.M., Entrepreneurship in Small Industries in Madurai City and its Environs, Sangam Publishers, Madras, 1975.

Sudip Chaudhuri, "Economic Reforms and Industrial Structure in India", *Economic and Political Weekly*, January 12th , 2002, Table 3.

Sukhpal Singh," Refugees as Entrepreneurs: The Case of the Indian Bicycle Industry," *The Journal of Entrepreneurship*, Vol.3, No.1, 1994.

Susumu Watanable, "Entrepreneurship and Small Enterprises in Japanese Manufacturing", *International Labour Review*, Vol.102, No.6, December 1970.

Tahera Mashauddin, "Personality Study of Successful and Unsuccessful Entrepreneurs", *Sedme*, June 1990.

Tandon.B.C, Environment and Entrepreneur, Chugh Publication, Allahabad, 1975.

Tapan K. Panda, "Entrepreneurial Success and Risk Perception Among Small-Scale Entrepreneurs of Eastern India, The *Journal and Entrepreneurship*, Sage Publications, New Delhi, July-December, 2002.

The Economic Times, 8th November, 2005.

Timberg Thomas A., Industrial Entrepreneurship Among the Trading Communities of Indial. How the Pattern Differs, Center for International Affairs, Development Advisory Service, Economic Development Report, No. 136, Harvard University, July, 1969.

Tyler, Sydney Scott, "Entrepreneurship and Small Business: A Strategic Management Front and Analysis", unpublished Ph.D, Syracuse University, 1996.

Udai Pareek and T.V. Rao, Counselling and Helping Entrepreneurs, *The Journal of Entrepreneurship*, Vol.4, January-June 1995.

Umesh Patnaik.C, "Entrepreneurship Education in Canada: An Observation," *Sedme*, Vol. 21, June 1994.

UNESCO Research Centre, Social Aspects of Small Industries in India: Studies in Hawrah and Bombay, UNESCO Research Centre on Social and Economic Development in Southern Asia, Delhi, 1962.

Vasant Desai, "Dynamics of Entrepreneurial Development and Management", Himalaya Publishing House, New Delhi, 2004.

Vasant Desai, Entrepreneurial Development, Himalaya Publishing House, Vol. 1, Bombay, 1991.

Vasudev Rao A.S., "Growth and Development of Small Enterprise Consultancy – Problems and Prospects" unpublished Ph.D, Karnataka University, Dharwad, 2003.

Venkata Rao, B.S, A Multidimensional Approach to Development of Entrepreneurship; Significance of Training and Others Inputs, SIET, 1994.

Venkatachalam,R. and Saleendran, P.T, Innovation & Entrepreneurship *Sedme*, Dec. 1990.

Vepa, Ram.K, Modern Small Industry in India, Sage Publications, New Delhi, 1988.

Vinayshil Gautham. "Towards Developing a Science and Technology based Entrepreneurship Index" in 'Technical Entrepreneurship : Issues of Research & Application' Ed. Vinayshil Gautham,Global Business Press, New Delhi, 1992.

Watanabe, Susumu, Entrepreneurship in Small Enterprises in Japanese Manufacturing, *International Labour Review*, Vol. 102, No. 6, December 1970.

William Diamond, Development Bank, The John Hopkins Press, Baltimore, 1957.

Yousif, A.Syigh, " Entrepreneurs of Lebanon: The Role of Business Leader in Developing Economy, Harvard University Press, Cambridge, 1962.

Yousif.A.Sayigh, "Cultural Problems and The Economic Development of the Arab World", in Bellah.R.N(ed), Religion and Progress in Modern Asia, The Free Press, New York,1965.